Anticipation...
waiting ~~for~~ the end.

For Andie Brum —
God bless you!
James T. Mayer, Jr.
1 Thess. 4:13-18

Anticipation...
waiting ~~for~~ the end.

Jimmy Draper

P.O. Box 1655 • Keller, Tx. 76244 • 800.856.8886

"Anticipation"

© Copyright 1999 • HeartSpring Media
All rights reserved
ISBN: 1-58695-000-2
Library of Congress Catalog Number: 82-74131
Reprint Edition, HeartSpring Media, October 1999
Printed in the United States of America

Unless otherwise noted, all Scripture quotations are used by permission
from one or more of the following versions:
- King James Version (KJV)
- American Standard Version (ASV)
- The Living Bible (© 1971 Tyndale House Publishers)
- "Phillips" (The New Testament in Modern English, Revised Edition,
  © J.B. Phillips 1958, 1960, 1972)
- "Wuest" (The New Testament: An Expanded Translation by
  Kenneth S. Wuest, © 1961 Wm. B. Eerdmans Publishing Co.)

HeartSpring Media
P.O. Box 1655
Keller, Texas 76244
1-800-856-8886

DEDICATION

To Finis and Lucille Floyd
Whose love produced my wife, Carol Ann,
and whose example of godliness
brightens my life daily.

CONTENTS

1 THESSALONIANS

1. THE GRACE OF GRATITUDE *1:1-4* 11
2. THE POWER OF THE GOSPEL *1:5-7* 21
3. THE CHURCH'S REPUTATION *1:8-10* 29
4. GENUINE GENTLENESS *2:1-8* 37
5. THE DEMANDS OF THE GOSPEL *2:9, 10* 45
6. BRINGING JOY TO GOD *2:11, 12* 53
7. OPPOSITION TO THE TRUTH *2:13-16* 61
8. OUR CROWN OF REJOICING *2:17-20* 69
9. SUFFERING TRIBULATION *3:1-5* 77
10. CHERISHED IN THE FAITH *3:6-10* 83
11. ABOUNDING IN LOVE *3:11-13* 91
12. THE WILL OF GOD *4:1-6* 99
13. CALLED UNTO HOLINESS *4:7-12* 109
14. THE COMING OF THE LORD *4:13-18* 117
15. A THIEF IN THE NIGHT *5:1-8* 127

16 AVOIDING THE DAY OF WRATH *5:9-11*   137
17 WHOLEHEARTED LOVE *5:12-15*   145
18 URGENT ADMONITIONS *5:16-22*   151
19 COMPLETE DEVOTION TO GOD *5:23-28*   159

2 THESSALONIANS

20 A GROWING FAITH *1:1-4*   169
21 THE RIGHTEOUS JUDGMENT OF GOD *1:5-10*   175
22 GLORIFYING THE NAME OF JESUS *1:11, 12*   183
23 THE GREAT APOSTASY *2:1-3a*   189
24 THE ANTICHRIST *2:3b-10*   197
25 BELIEVING A LIE *2:11, 12*   207
26 CALLED BY THE GOSPEL *2:13, 14*   215
27 STANDING TALL FOR GOD *2:15-17*   225
28 PRAYING FOR EACH OTHER *3:1-5*   231
29 AN EXAMPLE TO FOLLOW *3:6-9*   237
30 THE NECESSITY OF WORK *3:10-13*   243
31 ADMONISHING A BROTHER *3:14-18*   249

1 THESSALONIANS

The Grace of Gratitude
First Thessalonians 1:1-4

First Thessalonians is likely the first epistle that the Apostle Paul wrote, though some think that Galatians was penned just prior to its writing. Certainly it is among the earliest of his writings, and more important, is a significant revelation from God.

We need some background material if we are to understand and fully appreciate what is revealed. In Acts 6, we find that God led the Apostle Paul to Troas. While there he saw a vision, in which a man standing in Macedonia called, "Come over and help us." God spoke to Paul through this vision, and the great apostle obediently left Troas and went to Macedonia.

He proceeded to Philippi where his ministry didn't fulfill man's usual idea of success. In fact, he and Silas were beaten and cast into jail. While they were in chains, a great earthquake occurred. Their chains fell free and they could have escaped, but their refusal to leave led the jailer to cry for salvation. Paul declared, "Believe on the Lord Jesus and you will be saved, and your entire household" (Acts 16:31). After the conversion of the Philippian jailer, Paul and Silas were hurried out of town.

They passed through Appolonia and Amphipolis, but there is no word in the Bible that they preached in these cities. Then they moved on to Thessalonica, one of the most important cities in all of Macedonia. Running through the city of Thessalonica was the Egnatian Way, a superhighway of that day, tying the east and west together. There is no place in all of early Christendom that was more significant for the spreading of the gospel than Thessalonica. A church planted there could extend its message to the east and west, even to Rome itself. This is precisely what happened.

In Thessalonica, the apostle experienced both tremendous success and great opposition. He went to the synagogue, which was his pattern, and told the worshipers about Jesus Christ. He was there for three Sabbaths. Some think that was the entire length of time he was in Thessalonica. It may have been slightly longer, as the three Sabbaths may refer just to the length of time he was in the synagogue. At most, he was there only a few months.

At any rate, Paul was ejected from Thessalonica. There was a raid on the house of Jason, who was reported to be housing Paul and Silas (Acts 17:5, 6). They tore the town up trying to find Paul and Silas, who were rushed out of town.

So Paul preached a brief period of time in one of the most significant cities in all of Macedonia. He then moved on to Athens and then to Corinth. Every indication is that Paul was a very discouraged man when he got to Corinth. "I came to you in weakness—timid and trembling" (1 Cor. 2:3).

He had been chased from the last three cities he had visited, and those who opposed him did not simply content themselves with running him out of town. They followed him and made sure he encountered opposition in the next town. At Athens he was not run out of town, he was just ridiculed. That may be even worse than open hostility.

Now he found himself in Corinth, apparently a discouraged, worried man. Would the converts in Thessalonica stand? Would the opposition they were getting cause them to give up their faith? Would they revert back to their pagan religions, abandoning their faith in Christ? He had no way of knowing. His heart was concerned for the new church he had established in Thessalonica.

While in Corinth one of his companions, Timothy, brought him a report from Thessalonica. And what a report it was! The church in Thessalonica was strong. They loved him and were concerned for his well-being. They wanted him to hurry back and be with them. They were standing true in the face of persecution and opposition. The report brought Paul joy.

But there were problems in Thessalonica too. For one thing, they had the doctrine of Christ's second coming all confused. Some of them thought the second coming was so near that they shouldn't keep working. They determined to quit their jobs and let others feed them until the Lord came and took them off to glory. That is

*The Grace
of Gratitude*

why we find such statements as, "He who does not work shall not eat" (2 Thess. 3:10).

Also, some thought that since some of the people had died, they might miss the second coming. They asked, "What is going to happen to these dead believers? Are they going to miss out on the wonderful kingdom of God?" We can thus understand why Paul said to them, "I can tell you this directly from the Lord: that we who are still living when the Lord returns will not rise to meet him ahead of those who are in their graves. For the Lord himself will come down from heaven with a mighty shout and with the soul-stirring cry of the archangel and the great trumpet-call of God. And the believers who are dead will be the first to rise to meet the Lord" (1 Thess. 4:15, 16).

There were also those in Thessalonica who were slandering Paul, telling the people that he was just a heartless wanderer with no interest or concern for them. Thus, we can understand some of the things Paul said to undergird his love, concern, and interest toward them. There were also divisions in the church, and Paul needed to encourage them toward needed unity in the church.

There was also the danger that they might lapse back into their pagan immorality. They were all new Christians, and some of the people began to be offended because some of the leaders were not particularly tactful. The apostle encouraged them to respect their leaders, not only for themselves but for the position they held.

First Thessalonians is a letter of joy, a love letter to a group of people who are new in their faith. Paul writes to undergird their faith, to challenge them to remain

FIRST THESSALONIANS 1:1-4

faithful in their persecution and opposition. It is a wonderful revelation from the heart of God through the heart of the apostle to these new converts.

The first four verses form the greeting of this letter. The pattern of that day was to identify the writer first and then identify the person or persons to whom the letter is written. Then would follow a special greeting. Usually the greeting was coupled with some wish or some concern that God, or more often pagan gods, would smile upon the person receiving the letter. The content of the letter then followed.

This letter of Paul takes this standard form. Paul first identified himself and his two companions. Silvanus is likely Silas, according to Luke's record in Acts, Silvanus being the Greek name for Silas. Timothy we are familiar with. Paul has said a great deal about him in his writings.

THE POSITION OF THE CHURCH
Paul wrote to the *church* at Thessalonica. The Greek word for church is *ekklesia*, "those who are called out, those who are called for a special purpose." The Apostle Peter explains, "You have been chosen by God himself—you are priests of the King, you are holy and pure, you are God's very own—all this so that you may show to others how God called you out of the darkness into his wonderful light" (1 Pet. 2:9). The church consists of believers who have been called out of sinfulness into holiness, into God's own character. We are called-out ones.

He identifies the church as being "in God the Father

and in the Lord Jesus Christ" (1:1, KJV). The position of the church is in God and in Christ. It is not simply a group of people who believe in God, but a group of people who take their very being from him. They live and move and have their being in him. God is the atmosphere of the church. God's presence is the life of the church.

The title that Paul gives to Jesus, "the Lord Jesus Christ," is breathtaking. He is Lord, Jesus, and Christ. "Lord" is the Greek equivalent of the Old Testament Hebrew word, "Jehovah." It is always applied in the Old Testament to God. When Paul, who was a Jew of the Jews, called Jesus "Lord," he was ascribing to him all of the characteristics of God. Jesus is God. Everything that God is, Jesus is.

Then he is called "Jesus," his human name, meaning "Savior." He is called Jesus because he will save his people from their sins (Matt. 1:21). Paul was underscoring the fact that there is no one else by whom we can be saved.

The name "Christ" is the Greek word for Messiah. He is given this official title as the One who is the mediator between God and men. He is the One that God promised would come. He is the Lord Jesus Christ. Let us never forget that in these simple greetings and in these casual words that we often take for granted is a world of theology and truth. Let us never forget that our Savior is the Lord. Let us never forget that he is Jesus. Let us never forget that he is the Christ.

"May blessing and peace of heart be your rich gifts from God our Father, and from Jesus Christ our Lord" (1:1). God's grace brings forgiveness, joy, and delight to the human heart. Grace is always accompanied by peace. When we have God's grace, we have God's peace. The word "peace" means more than the absence of strife. In our day if we talk about peace, we generally refer to the absence of fighting or turmoil. To the early Christian, the word "peace" meant the prospering of the soul, a heart that is whole and complete. It carried with it the idea of prospering in all things, being happy and fulfilled. When God's grace is poured out on us, we will have a wonderful, prosperous, happy fulfillment within us.

THE PRAYER FOR THE CHURCH

"We always thank God for you and pray for you constantly. We never forget your loving deeds as we talk to our God and Father about you..." (1:2, 3).

The apostle prayed daily for the saints in Thessalonica. It was a daily commitment to God. He thanked God for what he was doing in believers' lives.

The word "thanks" (KJV) comes from a root Greek word, *eucharisto*, which means "grace." We have an English word that comes from the Greek, "eucharist" or "thanksgiving." He is declaring that they were thanking God every day for the fruits of grace that were revealed in the Thessalonians' lives.

Many scholars feel that Paul is saying here, "We think of each of you individually and call your name one by one before God." Their prayers were not vague. This was specific praying.

"We pray for you constantly" tells us that their praying

was a continuous thing. There was never any end to it. There was always a rejoicing in the work of God in the believers' lives, always prayer ascending in their behalf.

THE PERFORMANCE OF THE CHURCH
"Remembering without ceasing your work of faith, and labor of love and patience of hope..." (1:3, KJV). The "work of faith" simply refers to the work that God does in our lives because of our faith. That doesn't refer to helping little old ladies across the street, giving to the United Fund, etc. He is describing a work that faith promotes, a work that comes because of our relationship with Christ. Specifically, he is referring to the work of God's grace.

A "labor of love" is an extension of the work of faith. The word "labor" is a strong word, meaning "labor to the point of weariness," until we are exhausted. The Greek word for love is *agape*, a distinctively Christian term seldom used in the pagan world. Christians, under the leadership of the Holy Spirit, took *agape*, God's love, and applied it to the church. Coupled with the word "labor," it simply means self-giving to exhaustion. The Thessalonians did not serve because of what they could get out of it, but because of what they could give to those around them. Their labor was not dependent on others' praise. Because God had loved them, they loved—tirelessly and unceasingly.

"Patience of hope" literally means "hopeful patience." It does not mean a fatalistic resignation about what is going to happen, but refers to steadfast, resolute attention to the important things, priorities. It means giving ourselves to the things that really count and doing it with hopefulness.

When Alexander the Great began his great crusade to conquer the world, he gave all his property to his friends. Someone said, "You are giving everything away?" He said, "No, I have kept my hope." If we have this patience of hope, we can endure anything, because we will be walking toward the dawn of God's light instead of toward the darkness of man's failures.

THE POSSESSION OF THE CHURCH
"We know that God has chosen you, dear brothers, much beloved of God" (1:4). The Apostle Paul uses the word "know." This is a clear statement of fact. Not only can you know you are saved, but I can know you are saved. Not only can I know that I am saved, but you can know that I am saved. There are revelations of character, certain expressions of God's grace in human personality that can prove beyond a shadow of a doubt that one belongs to God, evidence that says, "We can see that God has chosen you." The redeemed belong to God, and this is obvious to those who observe.

The most cherished phrase that the Hebrews gave to their great men was the phrase "beloved of God." They only applied it to great leaders such as Moses, Solomon, Abraham, and to the nation itself. Paul says, "You are beloved of God." The greatest privilege of the great men

*The Grace
of Gratitude*

of Israel is now bestowed upon the humblest of believers.

Paul also called them "dear brothers." How much Paul loved that term. Paul used this phrase twenty-one times in First and Second Thessalonians. It had special meaning to the early church because the church represented a cross section of pagan society. There were Gentiles, Jews, rich people, poor people, master, slaves. But in Christ they were brothers. No one was more significant than another in the church. The great equalizer, God's grace, had brought them together. In the church they were all beloved of God. The possession of the church is the brotherhood of all who have received God's grace.

In Romans Paul explains this matter of God's choosing us, also called election. "For from the very beginning God decided that those who came to him—and all along he knew who would—should become like his Son, so that his Son would be the First, with many brothers. And having chosen us, he called us to come to him; and when we came, he declared us 'not guilty,' filled us with Christ's goodness, gave us right standing with himself, and promised us his glory" (Rom. 8:29, 30).

God's election simply means that salvation is in God's hand. We would never desire salvation without God's initiative, his Spirit revealing himself to man, moving in the heart of man. From man's perspective, whosoever will may come. God's choosing is based upon his knowledge of who will respond. "He is waiting, for the good reason that he is not willing that any should perish, and he is giving more time for sinners to repent" (2 Pet. 3:9). The election is made secure by personal response to the call of God in our lives.

2
The Power of the Gospel
First Thessalonians 1:5-7

Paul has already expressed the confident assurance he had of the Thessalonian believers' relationship with Jesus Christ. Now he tells them why he feels that way. "For when we brought you the Good News, it was not just meaningless chatter to you; no, you listened with great interest. What we told you produced a powerful effect upon you, for the Holy Spirit gave you great and full assurance that what we said was true. And you know how our very lives were further proof to you of the truth of our message. So you became our followers and the Lord's; for you received our message with joy from the Holy Spirit in spite of the trials and sorrows it brought you. Then you yourselves became an example to all the other Christians in Greece" (1:5-7). The evidence in their lives and their response to the gospel shows that they are part of the elect.

THE PRESENTATION OF THE GOSPEL
"We brought you the Good News." The gospel was presented. Some might feel that it was presumptuous for

him to say "our gospel" (KJV). In the New Testament the gospel is generally referred to as the gospel of the Lord Jesus Christ, but not here. We cannot proclaim a truth until we have experienced that truth. It must be *our* gospel. Paul, Silas, and Timothy had experienced the touch of God upon their lives. They had experienced the love of God in their hearts. They had embraced the truth of the gospel. It was a message of their own experience that they were delivering to the people. They had received the gospel, and then delivered it to the Thessalonians.

Paul recalls that the gospel did not come in mere words, but in power. They did not just give lip service to truth; God's power fell upon the people. There was a moving of the miraculous, supernatural power of God.

It is interesting that Paul says, "our gospel came unto you not in *word* only" (KJV), singular. It literally ought to read, "Not by mere discourse." In other words, it was not just by a presentation of a message that the gospel was given. There was truth to be sure. Certainly there was information given, but that wasn't all. There was God's power in their lives.

The Apostle Paul spoke several times about this power of the gospel. "And my preaching was very plain, not with a lot of oratory and human wisdom, but the Holy Spirit's power was in my words, proving to those who heard them that the message was from God" (1 Cor. 2:4).

That word "power" (KJV) is the Greek word *dunamis*. We get our English word "dynamite" from it. The dynamite of the gospel is more exciting than physical dynamite because all physical dynamite can do is tear something apart. But God's gospel has a constructive power about it. It doesn't explode or tear down, but builds and blesses.

Notice also that Paul ties that power to the Holy Spirit. It was a moving of the Spirit of God, not the power of man's personality. The thing that I long for in my presentation of the gospel is that God's Holy Spirit might do some things that cannot be explained any other way, things that cannot be explained except by saying that God did it.

Paul adds that the gospel came "in much assurance" (KJV). Some have concluded from this that when he preached the gospel and people were saved, they had assurance that they were saved. Actually what Paul is saying is, "When I preached to you, I had the confident assurance that God was in it. And when you were saved, I had the great assurance that you belonged to God." The assurance came to the preacher as he proclaimed the message. There was a quiet confidence, a great assurance that God was stirring hearts, that God was bringing redemption and salvation.

Notice the last part of verse 5: "And you know how our very lives were further proof to you of the truth of our message." Throughout 1 Thessalonians Paul is going to remind them of the example of the preacher. If any of us are going to be effective in preaching and sharing the gospel, it must be confirmed by fruit in our own lives. There were many charlatans in the ancient world, traveling religious philosophers who made their living defrauding the people. They had a ministry just for what they could get out of it. Paul said, "We didn't come like that. We didn't come for our sake, but for yours. We didn't come to enrich ourselves, but you, through the preaching of the gospel."

If our witness is to be believable, it must be the testimony of a life that is believable. There must be in our hearts, lives, and message evidence that God has done a work in our lives. There are a lot of people whose lives are defeated and barren, who talk a lot about religious things, but give no evidence of a relationship with Jesus Christ. Such a witness and testimony will bring no fruit.

THE PROGRESSION OF THE GOSPEL

When one is saved, where does he go from there? What is God going to do with him next? Is God only interested in getting us saved? Christian leaders, and preachers in particular, have greatly hampered true Christianity by leaving the impression that God is primarily interested in "getting people saved."

God is not through with us when we come to Christ. He is just starting with us. Birth (and new birth) is a beginning, not an end. Spiritual birth must be followed by growth and maturity.

Paul says, "You became our followers and the Lord's." The word "followers" really means "imitators." It refers to a mimic. In fact, we get our word "mimicking" from the Greek word. When we receive the gospel, we begin to imitate our spiritual leaders and the Lord. We try to live like they live. We imitate those who led us to Christ.

Some express astonishment that he says they were

imitators "of us" and "of the Lord" (KJV), putting "of us" first. We would swell up with indignation and say, "Oh no, you ought to follow God first." But we don't see God first. We first see the person who brings us the gospel. Paul is telling us, "Since we were the ones that delivered the message you started out imitating us, but you went on to imitate our Lord." That is the way it ought to be. God help us to be so transparent that people will imitate him as they imitate us, that they will be led past the vessel to the one who presents the eternal truth, even God himself.

"You received our message with joy." This is a beautiful picture of receiving something with delight, latching on to it hungrily and happily. They received the word "in spite of trials and sorrows." These new converts had to break away from pagan religions. Some of them had to leave the Jewish synagogue. They received a great deal of condemnation. "Trials and sorrows" is a phrase based on a word meaning "great pressure." It wasn't just mild opposition they faced, but tremendous strain.

Joy and affliction do not go together in our thinking. When we are afflicted, we are not happy about it. When we have great pressure brought upon us, it is not natural to have joy. But if Jesus Christ lives in our lives, he wants the gospel to progress in us until we receive the affliction, the persecution, the pressure, the discouragement, the frustration with joy.

"The fruit of the Spirit is joy" (Gal. 5:22, KJV). It is unnatural for us to react to pain with joy. Only the working of the Holy Spirit can produce it. The Holy Spirit is the reason we can have pressure and be happy. The Holy

Spirit is the reason we can have tragedy and rejoice in the midst of it. We can react to affliction, pain, and suffering with joy because of the Holy Spirit within us.

THE PATTERN OF THE GOSPEL
"Then you yourselves became an example to all other Christians in Greece." The word "example" is the Greek word which refers to a pattern. It first meant the imprint of a hammer on an object such as wood or brass, and then came to refer to the imprint of a seal. Ultimately it also signified a pattern.

"You became an example" is singular in the Greek. Individually the Thessalonian believers had become imitators of Paul and thus of Christ. But together, as a church, they became a single pattern to all who believed in Greece. They were a pattern community. People would see them and say, "If we just loved each other like that! If we could just forgive each other like that! Oh, if we could just live like that!"

God's Spirit in us has made us a pattern community. We react and respond to each other and to needs in a unique fashion. Thus we can be the best example of what God can do, a pattern for all the world to see. That is what I want for my life and for my church. We do not have any choice whether we are going to face affliction, opposition, or discouragement. But as the power of God manifests itself in our lives, as we become imitators of Christ, we will respond to affliction with joy. Thus, we become a pattern for what every church should be, a community within the community, reacting to tragedy and differences in a spirit that astonishes the world. We are a pattern to them of what they ought to be.

3

The
Church's
Reputation
*First
Thessalonians
1:8-10*

Every church and individual has a reputation. But what kind of reputation is it? What word comes from God's people? What witness is given in the community? "And now the Word of the Lord has spread out from you to others everywhere, far beyond your boundaries, for wherever we go we find people telling us about your remarkable faith in God. We don't need to tell them about it, for they keep telling us about the wonderful welcome you gave us, and how you turned away from your idols to God so that now the living and true God only is your Master. And they speak of how you are looking forward to the return of God's Son from heaven —Jesus, whom God brought back to life—and he is our only Savior from God's terrible anger against sin" (1:8-10).

There is so much in these verses that is appropriate for our consideration. If you desire to know what it means to be converted, look at these verses. If you want to know how a converted person is to live, study these verses. If

*The Church's
Reputation*

you want to know what kind of witness ought to come from God's people to the world, see these verses.

THE REPORT
The reputation of these people had spread far and wide (1:8). The Apostle Paul had a great ministry at Thessalonica. He ministered the Word of God there for just a short time, but hundreds of people were saved and a lively, vibrant church was established. Everywhere the Apostle Paul went, he wanted to tell about it. But he couldn't tell anybody about it because they already knew. In fact, they would begin telling him what had happened.

The phrase "spread out" comes from a word which refers to a trumpet blast or to a roll of thunder. It was not just a meek and mild reporting of something that took place, but a shouting at the top of their voices. The church is to be a trumpet declaring God's Word to a lost world.

The trumpet was used in various ways in Jewish worship services. For one thing, it was blown to gather people together when they desired to have special assemblies, etc. How much we need to sound the trumpet of God today calling people to worship, commitment, and dedication.

The jubilee trumpet was used when one was cleared of the death penalty or freed from slavery. Early in the morning of the first day of freedom from bondage, there was the sound of the trumpet. We need to sound the

FIRST THESSALONIANS 1:8-10

news that man can be freed from his sin through Jesus Christ.

The trumpet was also used to summon forces for war and to begin battle. How today the people of God need to sound the trumpet of war against evil, injustice, and sin and take a firm stand against the evil in our world.

The trumpet was also used when the people worshiped together. The beautiful melody of the trumpet would sound forth to expand the worship experience. There needs to be trumpeted from our lives, and from our churches, the wonderful truth of God. The moving message of love in a world of hate needs to be trumpeted forth. The Christians in Thessalonica shouted forth their relationship with Jesus Christ.

Remember that the great evangelistic crusade the Apostle Paul had in Thessalonica ended in a riot. A mob drove the evangelists out of the city. Common sense would have told these Christians, "Don't get too excited. You're liable to get in trouble if you don't keep your faith quiet." But rather than withdrawing into themselves, they went to the other extreme and boldly declared that Jesus Christ had changed their lives. They publicly declared their faith in him.

"And now the Word of the Lord has spread out from you to others everywhere." They were not reporting the word of man, but the Word of the Lord. In the original Greek this phrase, "Word of the Lord," means a word *from* God, not a word about God. God's very Word was trumpeted out through the people.

If we view the Bible as simply the word of man, as profound truth presented and recorded by dedicated men of another day, we will not be too excited about trumpeting the truth of its message. We need to realize that in the Bible God has literally given us a message from eternity, a message from heaven itself.

To be a Christian means we have received the Word of God in our lives. We have been transformed and are sharing with the world the Word of God which we have received.

REPENTANCE

"For they keep telling us about the wonderful welcome you gave us, and how you turned away from your idols to God so that now the living and true God only is your Master" (1:9). This verse gives us a beautiful description of genuine conversion.

"... how you turned away from your idols to God." That is the first step. Repentance declares, "I was going this way, but now am going this way. I once loved this, but now I love this." We always turn from idols to God in genuine repentance.

These people in Thessalonica grew up serving pagan gods. That is all they had known all their lives. It is hard to give up something we have held all our lives, but they turned from their pagan gods to the living God. When a man is converted, his life is changed. He breaks with the old way of life.

Verse 4 told us that we can know someone is saved. In verse 9, Paul declares that the reason we can tell that a person is saved is that his life has made a complete change. He has broken with the old life-style, and he is a new person, a new creation.

Paul explains it in 2 Corinthians 5:17, written about the same time as the letters to the Thessalonians. "When someone becomes a Christian he becomes a brand new person inside. He is not the same any more. A new life has begun!" The best way we can tell if we are saved is whether there has been a change in our lives. Has there been a breaking with an old way of life and a reorientation of thought? Is there a new commitment in our lives, a new way of living, a new way of thinking? Is there a new disposition and attitude toward life?

Some may say, "Well, we don't have any idols." Don't we? In the wilderness, they bowed down and worshiped the golden calf. Our idols may take the form of modern conveniences, or luxury, or public acclaim, or self-worship. We would be no more pitiful if we were to bow down before the grotesque form of a piece of wood in the darkest part of Africa, South America, or Asia than we would be in worshiping ourselves and our own ideas. Conversion is turning from our idols to God.

"You turned away from your idols to God so that now the living and true God only is your Master." There is a contrast here. Idols are dead; God is living. The idols are counterfeit; God is true. An idol has no ability to help; God can enter our lives and bring victory out of defeat, order out of chaos, blessing out of cursing.

Is your God real? You may say, "I belong to the church." That's not the question. Is your God real and genuine? Does he walk with you every day? There are many people who are turned off to church and religion.

But if we can get them past the ritual and help them find a God who is real, they will get so excited they will trumpet forth their faith. God is alive and active. Turning to that living God is genuine repentance.

THE RETURN

These Christians demonstrated their faith by their attitude toward Christ's coming. They were "looking forward to the return of God's Son from heaven" (1:10). These Christians in Thessalonica were waiting for God's Son to return. "Looking forward" is a Greek word that appears only here in the New Testament. It implies a readiness to welcome the person we are waiting for. There is a world of difference between waiting for someone with anticipation and waiting for someone with dread. This word indicates that these Christians were excited about Jesus' coming back again. They were ready to welcome the Master back. This anticipation encouraged them in the midst of persecution and pressure. Their dreams burst full and clear as they anxiously awaited Christ's return.

Even further, this rich Greek word also refers to trust and patience. Bear in mind that the Thessalonians had some wrong concepts about the second coming. Some said, "If he is going to come, there is no reason to work; let's just sit down and wait for him." That is why we will read later that Paul said, "He who does not work shall not eat." Patient waiting is not synonymous with idleness. The Thessalonian believers also had the fear that those who had died would miss the blessing of his return. In using this word, Paul was saying to them, "You must have the kind of faith that trusts God to keep his word, to do what he promised to do." We must not try to rush him or slow him down or try to chart his course for him. With trust and faith we must wait for his return.

I do not know when Jesus is coming back again. It could be today. But if his return is delayed, that is all right. We must be faithful and trust God to bring about the appearance of his Son in his own time. That is his concern, not ours. Our task is to work until he comes and be available to his Spirit.

Paul makes it very clear that he is talking about the historical Jesus, "whom God brought back to life, and he is our only Savior from God's terrible anger against sin." All of these words have such great significance. Jesus is the Savior, the one who delivers us from sin. We need to keep in the forefront of our minds and hearts that Jesus is always saving us, forgiving us, delivering us. That is what Jesus came to be for us.

Jesus can save us from every moment of anguish, envy, bitterness, resentment, and everything ungodly that comes into our lives. He can deliver us from it.

That doesn't mean that we won't have problems, but the problems will not have us. They may stalk us and attack us, but Jesus delivers us.

Jesus saves "from God's terrible anger against sin." We know that God is a God of love, but we need to understand that the other side of love is wrath. A holy God cannot tolerate evil. When we speak of the wrath of God, we are not speaking of a vindictive anger, such as we have. The wrath of God is a perfect wrath, not limited by human tendencies and limitations, never unjust, always right and equitable. It is a strong expression of the holiness of God reacting against evil. There will be an expression of God's wrath that will come upon this world and upon those who reject him. Jesus delivers us from that wrath.

Evil is not going to win. Sinfulness is not going to be crowned with ultimate success. Ungodly people are not always going to be in command. History is moving toward a time when God's wrath will be revealed from heaven. The scales will be balanced. The only way we escape such wrath is through Jesus Christ.

Genuine Gentleness
First Thessalonians 2:1-8

The Apostle Paul now reminds the Christians in Thessalonica of the manner in which he and his associates ministered among them, how deeply and gently they loved them. "You yourselves know, dear brothers, how worthwhile that visit was. You know how badly we had been treated at Philippi just before we came to you, and how much we suffered there. Yet God gave us the courage to boldly repeat the same message to you, even though we were surrounded by enemies. So you can see that we were not preaching with any false motives or evil purposes in mind; we were perfectly straightforward and sincere. For we speak as messengers from God, trusted by him to tell the truth; we change his message not one bit to suit the taste of those who hear it; for we serve God alone, who examines our hearts' deepest thoughts. Never once did we try to win you with flattery, as you very well know, and God knows we were not just pretending to be your friends so that you would give us money! As for praise, we have never asked for it from you or anyone else, although as apostles of Christ we certainly had a right to some honor from you. But we were as gentle among you as a mother feeding and caring for her own children. We loved you dearly—so dearly that we gave you not only God's message, but our own lives too" (2:1-8).

Here he calls to their attention the manner in which they came to Thessalonica. "For yourselves, brethren, know our entrance in unto you, that it was not in vain" (2:1, KJV). When the gospel was preached, people responded. There was a great ingathering of souls. It was not a futile effort. Hundreds, perhaps thousands, were saved. There was a great spirit of revival.

Paul proceeds to present a beautiful passage which shows that in our fellowship in the church a gracious gentleness ought to accompany our lives.

PRESENCE

"You yourselves know how worthwhile that visit was. You know how badly we had been treated at Philippi. ... Yet God gave us the courage to boldly repeat the same message to you" (2:1, 2). Here is a statement of the reality of the presence of God in their lives and ministry. Their boldness came from God. To the Apostle Paul, God was not just a concept that he accepted in his mind, but a Presence within which he lived. He moved in a constant awareness of the presence of God.

Then he says, "We were bold ... to speak unto you the gospel of God" (2:2, KJV). In 1:5 he called it "our gospel" (KJV), here God's. Is it the gospel of men or of God? It is both. It is God's in that it originates in him, but it is the gospel of men in that when a man believes and trusts God, God's Good News of salvation becomes his by experience.

The words "courage to boldly repeat" come from an interesting combination of two Greek words and literally mean "all speech." The formation of these two words into one word in the original means that their words flowed freely. There was no hindrance or hesitation, no stress or strain. The words simply flowed as a stream from their lips. In witnessing our words should come easily. We can talk easily about sports, politics, and business. But when we talk about God, we get tense and the words stumble on our tongue. We lack freedom.

Gospel preaching is often accompanied by hostility and opposition—"even though we were surrounded by enemies" ("with much contention," KJV). *Agone* is the Greek word here. We get our English word "agony" from it. It is a strong word. Wherever the gospel is preached, there will be people who oppose it. Wherever God's message is proclaimed, there will be those who do not like it. Paul is saying, "We had liberty through the presence of God even in the midst of agony and hostility."

PROCLAMATION

The word "preaching" (2:3) is the word *parakaleo*, "comforter." Jesus promised to send "another Comforter," the *paraklete* (John 14:16). The word literally means "to call alongside," to have someone beside you to help. Paul says, "Our preaching was a comfort and a help to you."

Paul's preaching was not based on deceit or "uncleanness" (2:3, KJV). That word refers to moral impurity, a charge often leveled at the early church by the pagan world. The early Christians often called the Lord's Supper a love feast. They spoke of greeting each other with a holy kiss. The Jews picked up on these terms of physical affection and began to accuse the Christians of sexual and moral impurity. The Apostle Paul denies that charge.

"We were allowed of God to be put in trust with the gospel, even so we speak; not as pleasing men, but God which trieth our hearts" (2:4, KJV). The words "were allowed" are from the same word as is translated "trieth." The literal translation is: "We were approved of God" and "God approves our hearts." The idea is really the same. To test someone, to prove them, is to approve them for a task. God never entrusts the gospel to anybody he does not test to see if they are sufficiently committed to present that gospel.

We must not carelessly present the gospel. God's purpose is to entrust the gospel to people who are committed with all their souls to presenting the gospel. God does not distribute his Word through an untested vessel. We are to please God, not men.

God looks on the inside of us, into our innermost beings, examining with careful scrutiny everything about us. Sometimes we can fool man, but we cannot fool God. God tests, tries, and proves our hearts. That is God's business. Men know what we do, but God knows why we do it. God knows the motive; men can only see action. God sees attitude; men see the externals.

"Never once did we try to win you with flattery" (2:5). "Flattery" literally means "to use a certain kind of speech to get something we want." Paul did not use ego-appealing words to get what he wanted, nor use a "cloak of covetousness" (KJV). The idea of a cloak is to conceal something. "Covetousness" does not simply mean greedy for money. It includes all selfish interests. Paul declares that they did not hide under a cloak of selfishness. Rather, they came in the power and presence of God.

He further reveals that they never endeavored to receive the praise of men. They did not claim superior authority over them, flaunting their credentials. They did not demand attention because they were apostles of Christ. Their presentation was not arrogant or selfish.

PRECIOUSNESS
"We were gentle among you. . . . We loved you dearly. . . . We gave you not only God's message, but our own lives too." The word "gentle" could be translated "babe." They were as gentle as a baby to them. They came in tenderness and love. They were as gentle as a mother "caring for her own children." A nurse who has charge of taking care of others' children is always very careful with them. But think of how especially tender and loving she is with her very own. "We loved you dearly" comes from a Greek word that is found only here in the New Testament. It describes faith, love, concern, com-

passion. "We gave you our own lives." That is in the imperfect tense and so means, "We gave our lives to you in the past and we keep on giving them." There is a continuous nature about it. Paul declares that they did not just give words, they gave themselves. They did not just give the doctrine of the Word of God, but they gave their own souls.

The Apostle Paul says, "When I told you the truth, I told you with my own soul, and I gave you not just words, but my own energy and strength."

The word translated "dearly" is an adjectival form of *agape*. This means to love like God loves. *Agape* love is God's love. It means to love unselfishly, sacrificially. It did not mean just to like others, or just to have a good relationship with someone, to be attracted to someone, but it meant to love so completely that you would give yourself for the other. Paul and his associates loved these new converts with a God-like love.

May God never let us get too big or busy for that. Whatever else we may say, whatever information we may impart, whatever doctrine we may proclaim, whatever ministry we may perform, may it always be wrapped up in an awareness of his love for us, our love for him, and our love for each other. The Thessalonians responded to the proclamation of the gospel because it was born out of a deep and abiding love that caused these missionaries to give their very lives for these new Christians.

We have to give ourselves to love with *agape* love. It cannot be just a matter of accepting certain things to be intellectually true or factual. It has to be a matter of giving ourselves to God as he has given himself to us. Then we are capable of giving ourselves to others.

We love God because he first loved us (1 John 4:10). We can go a step further and say that we love each other because he first loved us. We could not love each other otherwise. We are too different. Some of us are loud and boisterous, some quiet and gentle. Some of us are aggressive and enthusiastic, some of us are reticent and withdrawn. Some of us are young, and some are old. Some of us are conservative, some liberal. Some of us are wealthy, some are poor. Some are well-educated, some not educated at all. There is no way we can love each other without experiencing his love.

That is what blew the minds of the pagan world in the first century. In the church were master and slave, worshiping together. Here were people of different backgrounds bound together in love.

5

The Demands of the Gospel
First Thessalonians 2:9, 10

"Don't you remember, dear brothers, how hard we worked among you? Night and day we toiled and sweated to earn enough to live on so that our expenses would not be a burden to anyone there, as we preached God's Good News among you. You yourselves are our witnesses—as is God—that we have been pure and honest and faultless toward every one of you" (2:9, 10).

These verses underscore for us again the theme that runs constantly throughout the New Testament, a theme of fellowship in the church, love of the brethren, and the unity of purpose and spirit that should characterize the saints.

THE BOND

The word "brothers" was a very significant word to Christians in the first century. They were a very misunderstood, tormented, and persecuted group. They were from all walks of life, all ages, all backgrounds, all classes in society. But when they came together in the

*The Demands
of the Gospel*

church, they were able to worship together. This was a constant source of bewilderment to those who would criticize and attack the church. Within the church, brothers shared in a common cause together. There were many slaves and many masters in the early church. But when they came together to worship the Savior, they were just brothers in Christ. It is a beautiful thing to see people linking their hearts and lives together for a common cause and a common love. There is no stronger bond.

The Apostle Paul goes to great length to point out that they had worked night and day to pay their own way and provide for their own needs. People who work at a common labor or common pursuit have a bond through their work. Working together in a common setting, in a labor of toil, builds a strong tie of unity.

But there is also a spiritual bond, because they had all come from darkness to light, from death to life. They had shared the experience of forgiven sins. This bond bound their hearts together. Today we are often so busy fighting other Christians, we have forgotten who the enemy is. We feel so threatened by other groups of professing Christians that we have lost the understanding of the bond of Christian love. The early church shook the world, not because they were any more talented than we are, not because they were better educated than we are, not because they were better equipped and prepared than we are, but they shook the world because they had not yet learned to be competitors.

They really meant business in that early church. Some of them sold everything they owned so that others of them could eat. Some of them literally gave their lives rather than denounce their faith. They made an impact on the world that is still felt today.

THE BURDEN
"Night and day we toiled and sweated to earn enough to live on so that our expenses would not be a burden to anyone there." The word "toiled" comes from a word meaning "weariness." It describes work that results in physical tiredness. The word "sweated" comes from a root word which means "difficult." The idea is that they labored to overcome obstacles and difficulty.

Some accused Paul, Silas, and Timothy of coming to Thessalonica just to feather their own nest, to get something for their own support. The Apostle Paul says, "We worked hard, long hours, night and day, and with great weariness."

We need to remind ourselves that whatever work we do for God, he expects us to work energetically and give it our best. There is no room for laziness in the kingdom. There is no reason to rest on someone else's energy in the kingdom. We cannot let parents, husband, wife, children, or friends do the work for us. Paul and company worked to the point of physical exhaustion and still found time to preach the gospel. Why? So they would not be a burden to the Thessalonians.

Someone might ask, "Does that mean we shouldn't pay our pastor and church staff? Is it wrong to pay someone to do spiritual work?" Not at all. The Apostle Paul

The Demands
of the Gospel

himself sometimes received financial payment. In 1 Corinthians 9:4-12 he shows that God's ministers are entitled to financial assistance for their needs. Philippians 4:16 tells us that he received support from the church in Philippi while he was in Thessalonica.

Bear in mind that these Christian converts were babes in Christ in a pagan setting. They were used to charlatans and philosophers, traveling around making their pitch to the people, getting money and provisions and then moving on. It would have been a hindrance to the gospel had the apostles accepted anything from them, because they had not been there long enough for the people to understand their motivation. They needed to quickly show their sincerity by being willing to work and provide their own way.

This is a demonstration of a law that Paul said operated in his life: "All things are lawful for me, but all things are not expedient" (1 Cor. 6:12, KJV). There are some things that are permissible that we may forego because of the needs of the gospel.

The Apostle Paul considered himself a debtor to all men. He had a responsibility to all men. "I am made all things to all men, that I might by all means save some" (1 Cor. 9:22, KJV). It would have been inappropriate in that pagan setting in Thessalonica for him to demand that these new converts begin to provide his support. He rather worked hard so that he would not be a burden to those people.

He labored physically and preached the gospel of God. The word "preach" is the Greek word that means "to proclaim as a herald." It means to tell what one has been told. There are many things that are called preaching that are not preaching at all. God did not call us to proclaim our clever ideas, or to dream up cute ways of expressing his truth. He simply called us to deliver his message. God has said everything he desired to say and we do not need to talk about it or around it, but to proclaim it. To preach is to herald eternal truth.

THE BEHAVIOR
"You yourselves are our witnesses—as is God—that we have been pure and honest and faultless toward every one of you" (2:10). Paul is saying, "There are people who say we did not have our hearts right when we preached to you, that we took advantage of you, that we were coming to you to see what we could get from you. However, you know we poured our souls out for you."

It would be wonderful if we would all be very careful how we conduct ourselves toward each other. "Instead, be kind to each other, tenderhearted, forgiving one another, just as God has forgiven you because you belong to Christ" (Eph. 4:32). As we do this, the Christian bond is strengthened for the sharing of the gospel.

Belief behaves. We do not believe something if we do not do it, if our lives do not reflect it. Too many people say one thing but act another.

Because man's evaluation is faulty and we are prone

*The Demands
of the Gospel*

to misjudge, Paul adds, "as is God." God is a witness to what we are doing. Men see what we are doing, but God sees why. He looks at the heart.

When Samuel came to Bethlehem to anoint a new king from among the sons of Jesse (1 Sam. 16:1-13), he instructed Jesse to bring his sons before him one by one. The first one was a young man by the name of Eliab. Eliab was tall and good-looking. Samuel's response was, "Surely this is the man the Lord has chosen" (1 Sam. 16:6). God spoke to him and said, "Don't judge by a man's face or height, for this is not the one. I don't make decisions the way you do! Men judge by outward appearance, but I look at a man's thoughts and intentions" (1 Sam. 16:7). Our behavior is seen by men but judged by God. He knows why we behave the way we do.

Paul describes their behavior among the Thessalonians as "pure and honest and faultless." "Pure" simply means "separated unto God." They behaved as individuals who were not their own, but were bought with a price.

The word "honest" is the Greek word for righteousness and should be translated "righteously." Throughout the Word of God this refers to conformity to God's laws. It means to live as God tells us to live, according to God's commandments, according to the instructions of his Word. They also behaved faultlessly. They were irreproachable. There was nothing in their lives that would suggest criticism. They were an open book.

Let us underscore again that our lives relate to each other. We must live in such a way among those who believe that God is honored.

When we do that, God will begin to do something. When we begin to live like that, the world will beat down the doors of the church trying to get in. The trouble in many churches today is that the outsider looks in and sees viciousness, criticism, unkindness, and a lack of commitment. He sees people who live like the world and claim to know God, who very piously conduct themselves in spiritual matters, but impiously conduct themselves in other matters.

We are to live lives separated unto God, in conformity to his law, irreproachable among fellow believers.

Bringing Joy to God
First Thessalonians 2:11, 12

Once again the Apostle Paul asks the Christians in Thessalonica to remember how the missionaries had conducted themselves when they came there. "We talked to you as a father to his own children—don't you remember?—pleading with you, encouraging you and even demanding that your daily lives should not embarrass God, but bring joy to him who invited you into his kingdom to share his glory" (2:11, 12).

CONSOLATION
The Apostle Paul uses two words to describe the consolation he gave to them. "Pleading" is a word which can be translated "comforter." It is the same root word used to describe the Holy Spirit, the *paraklete*. It originally meant to call one alongside, to share something, to lift up and console. Nothing seems quite so bad when someone is there to help and strengthen us. Paul comforted the Thessalonians in the midst of their trials. He had told

them that God understood and would provide for every need in every pressure they faced.

"Encouraging" is closely related to the word "pleading." It specifically means to encourage someone in the face of great pressure and great opposition. These two words together paint a beautiful picture of the sympathy and consolation which the Apostle Paul and those who were with him had given to these Christians. It was as though they said, "God understands. God knows what you face. God has provided for you."

How much we need that today. How often we feel forsaken. How often we feel that no one understands. We need a word from God telling us that he understands. God has called one to stand by our side. God and his servants can lift us up, comfort, and strengthen us.

In every age, in every experience, in every need God has provided adequate consolation for us. Nothing that happens to us surprises God. Nothing happens to us that God can't turn around and make best for us. "And we know that all that happens to us is working for our good if we love God and are fitting into his plans" (Rom. 8:28). Nothing can separate us from the love of God. This is comfort indeed.

COMPASSION

"We talked to you as a father to his own children." That phrase is saturated with compassion and love. A father is truly concerned for his children. No father enjoys seeing his children discouraged or disappointed. There is always a yearning in the heart of a father to provide for his children. Such a spirit was in Paul's heart while he served in Thessalonica.

"Talked" referred to very solemn admonition and great seriousness. It literally meant "to call one as a witness." It is as though the Apostle Paul was saying, "We called God to witness what we told you." The truth given to them was of the utmost importance.

"We talked to you." "You" is singular. The King James Version says, "every one of you." The apostles had done much personal witnessing and counseling with them, in many instances dealing one by one with these new Christians.

Our greatest opportunities in the Christian faith involve personal relationships. It is wonderful to worship together, but this can never take the place of personal fellowship. The church must provide many opportunities to have that kind of intimate, personal relationship.

THE CHALLENGE

Why did Paul do what he did in Thessalonica? Why do we do what we do in our churches and ministries?

We must remember that these things are not ends in themselves. Every means of spreading the gospel and ministering to people is a means to an end, which is "... that your daily lives should not embarrass God, but bring joy to him who invited you into his kingdom to share his glory" (2:12).

The Thessalonians had been saved by a marvelous

God. They had received the Word of God in all of its beauty and splendor, but all that they received demanded something of them. There is a word in verse 12 in the Greek that does not appear in the English. Tucked away right at the first of the verse in the Greek New Testament is the word for witness, *martuse*. It is the same word that the apostles used in Acts 5 when they said, "We are witnesses of these things." The word means to give evidence so as to substantiate a claim, to give testimony so as to prove something. A witness proves by his life that what he says is true. Our lives are to be conclusive evidence of our faith. That word does not appear in the English translation; yet it is the most significant word in the verse.

Paul is saying, "The reason we gave ourselves to you, loved you, preached to you, worked day and night, exhorting and comforting and challenging you, was that you might learn by our witness and testimony that you serve a worthy God. That is the purpose of what we do."

If what we believe in our souls, if the commitments we have made to Christ do not affect how we live, something is seriously wrong. It does not matter how good we appear in public worship. If we lie and cheat, if we are abusive of those about us, then we are an insult to God and to others.

We who have been ministered to by the Spirit of God, through God's servants and saints, ought to prove by our lives that we have responded to God's claims.

A man is saved by grace plus nothing. However, once we have been saved there are many things God wants to do through us. If he is not working through us, then in some way our relationship with God is not right.

What did all this mean to people who were outcasts, in a day when it was illegal to worship the Lord? What did it mean to a man who might lose his life or his livelihood if he admitted being a Christian? What did it mean to live lives that would not embarrass God?

It meant perseverance in the midst of persecution. One great problem today is that we are Christians only incidentally. We are Americans, men, women, young, old, educated, uneducated, skilled, unskilled, oh, and by the way, we are Christians. To the Thessalonians Christianity was life! Even to admit that they belonged to Jesus Christ might cost them their lives. Christianity was not just something they practiced on Sunday. No matter what pressure bore down on them, they stood firm for Jesus Christ.

We think we have many pressures, but the truth is that we are not serious enough about Christianity as a life. The Thessalonian believers might see their children killed, their wives put to death, or their parents slain because of their faith in Christ. Yet they persevered. How pitiful our excuses are and how little we do for God!

The Thessalonians also experienced joy in the midst of sorrow. That is, they faced sorrow joyfully. We are walking through the inequities, the unfairness, and the sad moments of this life into a glorious eternity. Also, God has provided abundantly for our needs now. Paul's primary emphasis, though, is that by obeying God we bring him great joy.

THE CALLING

Now Paul moves from what we can do for God to what God does for us. We can never do as much for God as he does for us—"....him who invited you into his kingdom to share his glory." In English that looks like past tense, but in the original language it is present tense, the timeless present which speaks of continuous action. God calls us and he keeps on calling us. God is not through with us.

Paul links the kingdom of God with the glory of God. The kingdom of God is the operation of God's controlling and ruling power in and through the lives of his people. The kingdom of God is not only a realm, such as the kingdom of Great Britain, or a place (though it will be a literal kingdom when Christ returns). The kingdom of God is a happening, something that God is doing. We will never fully realize the kingdom of God until we stand in his glory with him in eternity, but we have the opportunity to be a part of God's kingdom now.

We do not have to work to bring people into God's kingdom. God does that. We do not work to bring in the kingdom; we are brought into the kingdom. We are brought to the place where God can work his life and his miracles through us. We are saved by our glorious God now and also have a foretaste of what eternity will be like.

The Greek for "glory" is the word from which we get "doxology." It originally meant an opinion, then a very high opinion. Gradually it came to be almost entirely ascribed to God. It eventually denoted splendor and majesty, thus glory.

FIRST THESSALONIANS 2:11, 12

We have been called into God's kingdom, there to be under the dominion and power of the Holy Spirit and to share in his glory.

7
Opposition to the Truth
First Thessalonians 2:13-16

"And we will never stop thanking God for this: that when we preached to you, you didn't think of the words we spoke as being just our own, but you accepted what we said as the very Word of God—which, of course, it was—and it changed your lives when you believed it. And then, dear brothers, you suffered what the churches in Judea did, persecution from your own countrymen, just as they suffered from their own people the Jews. After they had killed their own prophets, they even executed the Lord Jesus; and now they have brutally persecuted us and driven us out. They are against both God and man, trying to keep us from preaching to the Gentiles for fear some might be saved; and so their sins continue to grow. But the anger of God has caught up with them at last" (2:13-16).

From the human standpoint, who was responsible for your salvation? Who was it that God used to witness to you? It may have been a parent, a brother or sister, a pastor, or a Sunday school teacher. Could that person whom God used to lead you to saving faith in Jesus Christ say, "Because of the way you responded to the Word, I thank God for you"?

Opposition to the Truth

THE RECEPTION OF TRUTH

We find the word "receive" twice in verse 13 (KJV), but it is two different words in the original language.

"Thank we God without ceasing, because, when ye received the word of God...." The word "received" there means "to hear." It refers to an objective receiving of information. "Ye received it... as the word of God...." The second word translated "received" means "to welcome, to receive with delight and joy." They heard it with their ears and responded with their hearts.

That is the way the gospel is always received. It first comes to us objectively, as an objective revelation about Jesus Christ. But the Word of God never changes our lives until it becomes subjective, until it becomes personal to us and we receive it with all of our heart.

It is all-important how we receive the truth of God. Spiritual conversion is not giving mental assent to certain principles as being right. Spiritual conversion is giving consent to the rule of Christ in our hearts.

Paul calls God's message "the word of God" and "not the word of men" (KJV). Paul probably would not have ranked very high on the after-dinner speakers' tour. Some of the greatest thinkers of all history came from the Greek culture, and the circumstances in which the gospel was preached would have made it easy for the Apostle Paul to accommodate himself to popular philosophies. But he spurned these, choosing to communicate the wisdom of God.

"The word of God... effectually worketh also in you" (KJV). "Worketh" in the New Testament always refers to supernatural activity, but it is not always applied to

God. Sometimes it is applied to Satan. Here Paul was saying, "It is the supernatural Word of God that is at work in you. God is doing it."

Many ask, "How can I be what I ought to be?" If we hear God's Word with our ears and commit our hearts and lives to it, God will work out his Word through us. We wonder why we get so frustrated trying to do right. It may be that we have not learned the secret of letting God work through us.

The word "believe" is in the present tense. It is not the tense of past action, which would refer to their conversion in the past. It is rather the present tense of continuous action. A commitment of life to God is a life that keeps on trusting, that keeps on applying faith. "The just shall live by faith" (Rom. 1:17, KJV). The reception of truth is to be a continuous experience.

THE RESULT OF THE TRUTH

What happens when we receive the truth of God? Everything will not necessarily run smoothly when we get saved. It will not all be peaches and cream. Everything is not going to go just as we want it to go. We will not suddenly be without problems. "And then, dear brothers, you suffered what the churches in Judea did, persecution from your own countrymen, just as they suffered from their own people the Jews" (2:14).

The result of the truth coming into the lives of the Christians of Thessalonica did not mean peace, but trouble. Their own neighbors, and perhaps their own

*Opposition
to the Truth*

families, began to persecute them. They found opposition at every turn in the road.

In some form, persecution will always come to the Christian. There will always be opposition to the working of God through us. Paul is simply and honestly saying, "You are walking where other saints have walked. You became saved and have been under persecution." When the gospel is received, there will always be opposition to it.

Persecution may come in the form of ridicule. Others may laugh at us and make fun of us. They may ostracize us and isolate us. Special pressures may be applied in the form of unfair demands and expectations. But persecution in some form will come.

The Thessalonians' persecution came from both Jews and pagans—"You suffered persecution from your own countrymen." This is simply a reminder for us that there will be persecution in and out of the church. Sometimes the most severe opposition to the working of God in our lives will come through people who claim to have had an experience with God.

While they shared a common persecution, they also shared a common comforter. "Ye, brethren, became followers of the churches of God which in Judea are in Christ Jesus" (KJV). We are in Christ. We live, move, and have our being in him. When we are persecuted, they are not persecuting us, but him. We wrestle not against flesh and blood, but against principalities and powers in high places. Wherever the opposition to the truth of God expresses itself, it is always an expression of the age-old conflict between evil and God.

FIRST THESSALONIANS 2:13-16

THE REBELLION AGAINST THE TRUTH

Notice the rebellion against truth in verses 15, 16. He lists the Jews' sins, and the consequences. They had no patience with anyone. They stoned the prophets. They killed "the Lord Jesus." "Lord" is his heavenly name, "Jesus" his earthly name. They killed the God-Man. Then they persecuted and opposed us. They thought they were persecuting us, killing Jesus, stoning the prophets, but they were fighting God.

Paul continues, "They please not God, and are contrary to all men" (KJV). Tacitus, an early historian in the Christian era, described the Jews as being a nation of people who were angry at the world. If we do not please God, we will be in conflict with others.

Further, they forbade Paul and the others to speak to the Gentiles so they could be saved. The Jews believed that they were God's people, which was certainly true. But they thought being God's chosen people was a privilege, rather than a responsibility. They never quite understood that they were chosen for service, not for their own glory. They were not chosen so they could be a superior people who lorded over everyone else because of their great position. They were chosen to be an instrument of God in reaching the world. It was always in God's heart to reach an entire world with the gospel. The Jews were to be his tool to bring that to pass. However, the Jews did not want the Gentiles to get the gospel and that was sin.

They continued to sin until they "fill up their sins always" (KJV). They committed every sin they could. And so God's wrath has come upon them to the utter-

Opposition to the Truth

most. That does not mean that God cut off the Jews, but the Jews stepped aside from God's purpose. "All Israel will be saved" (Rom. 11:26). But right now the wrath of God is upon her because of her rebellion against the truth.

It is one thing for us to read in a book how the Jews and the Gentiles in Jerusalem, Judea, and Thessalonica opposed the truth, but I would like to bring it a little closer to home for us today.

There are two very practical and personal ways in which we oppose the truth. The first is by opposition to what God is doing. There are people who fight everything God wants to achieve. They oppose God's leadership in the church. Anytime there is a spiritual goal to be achieved, or a spiritual direction set, they are always negative. They are always looking for something to be unhappy about. We oppose the truth when we make it difficult for God to do what he wants to do with his people.

What God does in our lives is often like surgery. The Word of God presses through our flimsy excuses. It tears away our hypocritical masks that we use to hide from each other. We oppose the truth when we do not give God liberty to work his way in our lives and in the lives of others even though it is often uncomfortable. And when we oppose what God is doing in his people, then we are actually opposing him.

The second way that we oppose the truth is by hindering the preaching of the Word by inconsistent participation in public services. Did you ever try to start a fire with wet or green wood? Dry wood requires seasoning and aging. The church is no different. The most difficult day of the year to have a worship service is Easter. On that day, we have much green wood.

We may be a hindrance by our very lack of attendance. We can also be hindrances if we do not listen. Preaching is 90 percent listening. It really is! If we do not get anything out of the message, it may be that we have not been listening. God will say something to us if we listen.

If we do not share financially in the ministry of the church, we hinder the gospel. We hinder the preaching of the gospel when we fail to share with our possessions in what God is doing through the church. In all these ways we oppose the truth.

Our Crown of Rejoicing
First Thessalonians 2:17-20

"Dear brothers, after we left you and had been away from you but a very little while (though our hearts never left you), we tried hard to come back to see you once more. We wanted very much to come and I, Paul, tried again and again, but Satan stopped us. For what is it we live for, that gives us hope and joy and is our proud reward and crown? It is you! Yes, you will bring us much joy as we stand together before our Lord Jesus Christ when he comes back again. For you are our trophy and joy" (2:17-20).

The Apostle Paul is writing to undergird his love for the Thessalonians and to assure them of his desires to be an encouragement and a help to them. It is interesting that one of the ways Satan always attacks the work of the ministry is at the point of motives. God does a great work and immediately there will be some who will question the motives of those involved. It was so in Thessalonica, and it has not changed a great deal over the years.

THE THROB OF LOVE

We cannot read these verses without being made aware of the tremendous love that the Apostle Paul had for these people. He begins by calling them "dear brothers," a phrase of tender affection. It refers to those who are beloved in the Lord and speaks of great compassion and concern. It is a biblical term applied uniquely to the Christian faith. It reminds us that we who claim the name of Christ are brothers and sisters in the faith. Much emotion vibrates from these words.

"After we left you" is one word in the original language. It literally means "to be torn away from." The root word means "to be orphaned, to suddenly lose parents, to be suddenly torn away from those who have borne you." It speaks of grief, bereavement, and loneliness. We need to recapture that kind of Christian fellowship, so that when we are taken from each other, even for a brief time, there is a sense of loss.

Notice Paul's statement, "though our hearts never left you." The world says, "Out of sight, out of mind." The Apostle Paul says, "You are out of sight, but you are loved more than ever. You are still in our hearts."

He continues, "We tried hard to come back to see you once more." In the Greek, "tried hard" speaks of haste and diligence. He seems to be saying, "We endeavored to do everything we could to get over the obstacles to come to you." He did not just exert token efforts to be with them. Rather he gave great effort, great energy, and great strength to come to them.

The word translated "desire" in the King James Version is a word that is often translated in the New Testament as "lust." It is usually a driving, uncontrollable passion to have something that is wrong. But here Paul is declaring, "There was in our hearts a fierce and uncontrollable urge to be by your side." He tried again and again to rejoin them. Here is the throb of love.

THE THRUST OF SATAN

"Satan stopped us." The thrust of Satan is always a hindrance to the work of God. The word translated "stopped" is a word which literally means "to cut up." It usually referred to cutting up the road to stop the advance of someone along the highway, to make it impassable so they could not reach their destination. Paul declares that Satan is out to throw up roadblocks in our way.

How did Satan stop them? Some think by illness. We know that the Apostle Paul was frail of body, and perhaps his stamina was not what it ought to be. Or it could have been that there was trouble in the other churches that he was serving. Because of the critical nature of these problems, he could not be free to come to be with them. It could also have been that the political/religious situation in Thessalonica made it impossible for him to return.

We do not know how Satan hindered them. The important thing for us to understand is that Satan does hinder God's servants. He thrusts obstacles in the way of God's people. Satan tears down and discourages, creates difficulties and depression. How he does it is insignificant, but he does it.

Our task is to move past Satan's barriers. God is still supreme. Satan does not do anything that surprises God. Satan may hinder us, but God's purposes are still achieved. Imagine how bleak the outlook for the Christian movement must have seemed to the early disciples when Jesus was nailed to the cross. Satan thought he had won the battle, but it was still within the providential purposes of God. The hand of God was guiding his hidden purposes to fruition despite the barrier Satan had erected. God always triumphs.

The battle is already won. Satan is a defeated foe. When Jesus Christ rose from the grave, he sealed Satan's doom. God is in control.

It is amazing that Satan would be so concerned about three humble missionaries. He didn't seem to be worried at all about Nero or other "important" people of that day. Yet he attacked three simple preachers. Satan's most dreaded foes, his worst enemies, are those who proclaim the gospel of Jesus Christ. Satan does not want the gospel preached. He does not want the message of forgiveness and grace to be presented to a dying world.

He does not mind if a group calls itself a church as long as it doesn't preach the gospel. But when people stand and declare the eternal truth of God, Satan will get busy. Indeed, if there are no storms from Satan, we should be concerned because if we never disturb Satan, we must not be pleasing God.

Satan always outsmarts himself. He is not as clever as he thinks. He knows more than we know, but he is ignorant compared to God. He always ends up running his head against a brick wall. Really, it is rather humorous. Think about Job, for instance. Here is a man who seemed upright in every way, a model citizen, one that we could look at and say, "That is the way a godly person ought to be." And yet he suffered every kind of injustice, every kind of misunderstanding. Without deserving it whatsoever, he lost his family and his wealth. His friends became suspicious of him and ridiculed him. Everything that could happen happened to him. And yet, had Job not been tested there would never have been a record of his faith for us who also suffer the pressures of Satan upon our souls. Satan thought surely he would win, but not so. Job has become an encouragement and an example to all of us. It is always that way. Through every trial and temptation, God will bring victory to his people.

Satan may think he has used up the energy of the church. But God is still working his purposes through us. He still has his hand on the throttle, and his hidden purpose will be achieved.

The question arises, "How can we know whether a certain circumstance is of Satan or of God?" At least twice in the book of Acts, the Apostle Paul had it in his heart to do something and God's Spirit stopped him. How do we know whether a hindrance is from God or Satan?

First, determine the intent of the hindrance. If the hindrance pulls against God's purpose in our lives, if it keeps us from being holy and useful, if it hinders us from growing and maturing, we can be sure it is a tool of Satan.

Also, if a hindrance pleases our physical, sensual self,

then it is of Satan. If it satisfies our ego, feeds our pride, satisfies our sensual self, then it is from Satan. If the hindrance is something contrary to our sensual nature, chances are that it is God cutting across some superfluous area of our lives, trimming off the rough edges to make us more fitted for the temple that God is building.

We can also tell if it is of Satan or God by the time in which it comes to us. Many times we may be praying or reading our Bibles and some lustful, blasphemous thought comes into our minds. That used to perplex me. There is a law of mental science that says that one thought leads to another thought, a thought builds upon the thoughts that have preceded it. One bit of knowledge helps us understand another bit of knowledge. But Satan's attacks are never like that. We can be going along a certain line of thought when out of a clear blue sky, something comes along that is completely irrelevant and opposed to what we have been thinking. That is Satan attacking our concentration and purpose.

THE THRONE OF CHRIST
"You will bring us much joy as we stand together before our Lord Jesus Christ when he comes back again" (2:19, 20). The Greek literally says, "Are not you in the presence or coming of our Lord Jesus Christ?" This word was used to designate the time a great person, perhaps a king, would spend at a place. In the New Testament, rather than simply meaning "a royal visit," the word

meant *"the* royal visit," the second coming of Christ. This is a picture of the returning, royal King upon his throne. Here is our Christ returning as victor.

We need to be reminded again of the authority of our Lord over Satan, the victory that is ours in Jesus Christ. Satan is a fraud, a phony, a counterfeit. He can only pretend. When Moses cast his rod upon the ground, it became a serpent. The magicians of Egypt also cast rods upon the ground and by sleight of hand or by some way of magic, they duplicated the sign. (But you will remember that Moses' serpent ate theirs!)

Also, Satan has never kept a promise and he never will. That is why the world reels in despair. The world has run the gamut of every sensual, earthly lust and desire but found no satisfaction there. Jesus is the returning Christ who comes in power and authority.

The apostle says, "When Jesus comes again, we are going to rejoice in you." One of the greatest joys that we shall ever know is the joy of seeing lives that God has allowed us to touch and help. The glory of any teacher is his pupils. The glory of any pastor is those who have come to know God through his preaching. When we stand before God at his throne, our crown of rejoicing will be those whose lives we have touched for him.

In the Greek there were two words for "crown." One meant a royal crown, another a victor's crown. In our struggle, we are a victor's crown. We are not poor, emaciated examples of godliness. We have been elected to God's grace and God has changed us. He will keep us and present us to himself as many crowns when he comes. That makes every effort expended and every energy worth it all. "You are our crown of rejoicing. You are our glory."

The word for "glory" is *doxa*, from which we get "doxology." Those Christians were the praise, joy, and glory of the great apostle. "Hallelujah," he said, "for what you are to us."

Absent? Apart in body, not in heart. Hindered? Not detoured. Discouraged, wondering sometimes if it is worth it? At his throne we shall be presented to each other and thus to our Lord as a crown of delight, rejoicing, and praise.

9
Suffering Tribulation
First Thessalonians 3:1-5

"Finally, when I could stand it no longer, I decided to stay alone in Athens and send Timothy, our brother and fellow worker, God's minister, to visit you to strengthen your faith and encourage you, and to keep you from becoming fainthearted in all the troubles you were going through. (But of course you know that such troubles are a part of God's plan for us Christians. Even while we were still with you we warned you ahead of time that suffering would soon come—and it did.) As I was saying, when I could bear the suspense no longer I sent Timothy to find out whether your faith was still strong. I was afraid that perhaps Satan had gotten the best of you and that all our work had been useless" (3:1-5).

One of the most difficult things for us to understand is why people suffer, why there are disappointments and despair, why we have afflictions of any kind. Why is there illness, tragedy, death?

In this passage we find grounds for rejoicing in spite of suffering.

*Suffering
Tribulation*

COMPASSION

Paul declared that he was sending Timothy, "our brother and fellow worker, God's minister." These are words of endearment. "Our brother" speaks of someone for whom we have great affection, someone in whom we have a great interest. He is our brother because we share a common faith. This shows the love that should exist between God's children.

Paul loved the young Christians at Thessalonica so deeply that he sent his most trusted adviser, his dearest friend, the one who walked by his side and encouraged him. Now he was left alone. Apparently the Apostle Paul had physical limitations and pressures. In addition, he was in a hostile city. Yet he sent his most trusted friend and co-worker because of his love for those people.

Here is compassion. He had deep love for the Thessalonians, and also for the lost because he stayed to preach the gospel in Athens while he sent Timothy to encourage and to establish those young Christians in Thessalonica. The prayer of our heart should be, "Lord, help us to love each other and those who need the touch of God upon their lives."

The word "minister" is our word "deacon," a servant, one who ministers.

CONCERN

"When I could stand it no longer, I decided to stay alone in Athens and send Timothy . . . to visit you to strengthen your faith and encourage you." This is Christian concern.

The King James Version says, "we thought it good." In the Greek "thought it good" is one word which means, "we were well pleased." It seemed to be the best thing to do. He was thrilled to send someone to minister to them. The Greek word is one that is filled with enthusiasm, excitement, emotion, and at the same time a steadfast purpose and high resolve. Paul was concerned so much for them that he was willing to be left alone. He was left apart from those who could minister to him in order that they might minister to others.

When the writer of Hebrews describes our pilgrimage on earth, he speaks of a great arena where we are engaged in the race of life that God has committed to us. "We are compassed about with so great a cloud of witnesses.... Looking unto Jesus, the author and finisher of our faith...." (Heb. 12:1, 2, KJV). Our Savior who poured his life into our salvation, who made it possible for us to be forgiven and to know him, is watching with intense interest what we are doing. More than that, the apostles and saints who have passed on to glory stand encamped about, watching, knowing that what they gave their lives for has been entrusted to us and they are interested in its further progress.

The great tragedy in American life today is that we are not concerned about anything. We complain a lot, but don't ask us to get involved, don't ask us to help make decisions. We are not really interested. We live in a day of apathy. We do not care.

Suffering Tribulation

"When I could stand it no longer, I decided to stay alone in Athens." The word translated "stay alone" means "to be abandoned." "It was better," Paul said, "for me to be lonely so you would be ministered to." The key to the Christian life is found in a statement Jesus made when the disciples quizzed him about greatness in the kingdom. He said, "I did not come to be served, but to serve" (Matt. 20:28). We often want someone to minister to us, to cater to us. We want someone to do things for us. But if our goal in life is to be ministered to, then we will be unhappy. The Apostle Paul said, "I was willing to be abandoned, orphaned, isolated in order for you to be ministered to."

What was Paul concerned about? The Thessalonian Christians' faith. He wanted them to be strong, growing, maturing. Our faith is about the last thing that most of us are concerned about. Most of us spend more time getting ready to come to church, shaving, washing, combing our hair, and dressing than we do preparing our souls to worship God. We need to care about our faith.

The words "that Satan had gotten the best of you" literally mean "that the deceiver had accused you." Satan wants to destroy us, so he tempts us, encourages us to do wrong, and then when we have done it accuses us of doing it. Satan wants us to do wrong so that he can laugh at us, ridicule us, and accuse us. He is "the Accuser of our brothers" (Rev. 12:10). He accuses us before God.

Paul was concerned because he knew we would have

Satan for an enemy. Like a roaring lion he goes about seeking whom he may devour. We need to be strong in the Lord, else we will be overwhelmed.

COMFORT
Paul sent Timothy to "strengthen your faith." "Strengthen" literally means "to build a support under something," to shore it up, put a foundation under it.

"Encourage" is the word which applies to the Holy Spirit, meaning to call someone alongside to encourage and strengthen. Put the two words together and you get something like, "I sent Timothy to you in order to build up your faith, to be sympathetic and encourage you."

Timothy was sent "to keep you from becoming fainthearted" (3:3). "Becoming fainthearted" is translated from a word that could be used to describe a dog wagging his tail. A dog will wag his tail in order to get something he wants. He may want us to pet him or to give him something.

Satan comes like that. He does not always come with a sword in his hand. Sometimes he comes as an angel of light to trick us. Paul declares, "I do not want you to be moved. I do not want Satan to beguile you with fair speech and flattering words, and thus cause you to go back on your commitment."

Concerning their troubles Paul declares, "But of course you know..." (3:3). In the Greek language the personal pronoun was shown as a separate word only when the subject was to be emphasized. Paul is saying, "You, yourselves know that when we were there we told you that we were all going to suffer tribulation."

The troubles are "appointed" (KJV) or unalterable. This refers to something that is so certain that it cannot be changed. The Apostle Paul is giving us a principle that we must understand, or else be swept away and beguiled by Satan. We cannot get around this fact: we will suffer, we will have tribulation, we will have persecution.

Whether it be physical illness, social disappointments, or personal pressures in our souls, we can count on suffering. We must not let it surprise us. Remember, God is still God, and Satan is a defeated foe. Do not let him bluff you. He has no power but that which God allows him to have. Walk in God's strength and power. When suffering threatens us to the point of despair, we can be sustained by walking with the Lord.

10
Cherished in the Faith
First Thessalonians 3:6-10

These verses display a tender love and fellowship between the Apostle Paul and the Christians at Thessalonica. Christian fellowship is the greatest tool in evangelism today. The greatest hindrance to winning people to Christ is not atheism, but the lack of unity, fellowship, and love within the church.

I am convinced that the church that is going to reach people for Christ must have a fellowship of love and compassion. When we have that, we will not have to worry about people being saved. They will come to us. They will want to know what we have. If we love each other, if there is a cherishing of Christian hearts bound together in the purposes of God, men will beat down the door of the church to get in. These verses underscore that tremendous truth.

Paul begins with a personal word. "And now Timothy has just returned and brings the welcome news that your faith and love are as strong as ever, and that you remember our visit with joy and want to see us just as much as we want to see you. So we are greatly comforted, dear brothers, in all of our own crushing troubles and suffering here, now that we know you are standing true to the Lord" (3:6, 7).

Notice the very warm, personal relationship in these verses. It is very interesting that Paul says, "Now when Timothy came from you unto us..." (3:6, KJV). Paul had sent Timothy to Thessalonica as his representative to them, but he came back as their representative to Paul. The bond of fellowship and unity transcended all personal loyalties that might exist between individuals and became a loyalty to God and the overriding purposes of the gospel.

In the Greek it literally says, "But when Timothy just came from you to us." The idea is that Timothy had just arrived, and now Paul is writing a letter to the Christians in Thessalonica. This is a reminder to us who are always prone to postpone writing important letters. Paul felt an urgency. This underscores the intense personal affection and the deep significance he attached to the relationship he had with these people.

Timothy returned with the "welcome news." These words are translated like this only here in relationship to the report of a church. Everywhere else the Greek word applied to preaching the gospel. It is literally "good news." The early church used only one word for the preaching of the gospel, and it was this word. The Apostle Paul was so delighted to get word of their faith and love that he says, "It was like the first preaching of the gospel to my soul." It shows the depth of feeling, compassion, and love that bound them together.

Then he continues, "You remember our visit with joy

and want to see us just as much as we want to see you." He was afraid they might not care for him, because they had been told that Paul did not care for them. He rejoices in their mutual love and the fond memories each cherished for the other.

He then calls them "dear brothers." Here again is that word of unity. They were glad to be brothers in a common cause. "Don't ever forget those wonderful days when you first learned about Christ. Remember how you kept right on with the Lord even though it meant terrible suffering. Sometimes you were laughed at and beaten, and sometimes you watched and sympathized with others suffering the same things. You suffered with those thrown into jail, and you were actually joyful when all you owned was taken from you, knowing that better things were awaiting you in heaven, things that would be yours forever" (Heb. 10:32-34). One of the reasons the early Christians suffered was that they would not remain anonymous when their friends were arrested and punished for being Christians. They turned themselves in and said, "We belong with them. We are one of them too." They brought trouble on themselves by standing up for Christ and identifying with God's people.

Today we have to beg people to identify with a church. They move to a new community and they visit churches, but are slow to join one. Paul calls the Thessalonian Christians "brethren," having a common purpose. Whenever Christian people will unite themselves together and faithfully serve our Lord, it is always good news of brothers joined in a common cause.

PURPOSE

He says, "For now we live, if ye stand fast in the Lord" (3:8, KJV). Here is Paul's purpose for life. In Philippians 1:21 (KJV) the Apostle Paul says, "For to me to live is Christ," and now he says that to really live is to see the faithfulness of the Thessalonian Christians. To him, serving Jesus did not mean sitting around thinking about Christ. It did not mean just studying and feeding his soul while everything else fell apart. Living for Christ meant serving him. Living for Christ meant preaching the gospel, reaching and serving those whom God had entrusted to him. It is not inconsistent for him to say his purpose in life is to live for Jesus Christ and for faithful service in the fellowship of the church. If we live for Jesus, we will live for each other. We will love each other just as God loves us.

Paul is declaring, "I live to see you grow in God." They had accused him of being mercenary and not being interested in them, but he revealed his deep love and concern for them in this statement. We are serving Christ and living for Christ when we allow Christ to touch another life through us.

There are many people in our day that always want to talk about Jesus. I am not against that, but I do get a little weary of people always talking about Jesus to each other and never sharing Christ with those outside their small circle. The whole purpose of the gospel and the church is God reaching through us. I do not know why God did it that way. Why did he not write a sign across the sky so men could read about it? Why did not God simply send angels to the four corners of the earth to be his messengers? I don't know! But I do know that God has chosen to use us. Our purpose and life ought to be to serve our Lord as he reaches through us to others.

Do not tell me how much you love Jesus if you do not love the brethren. Do not tell me how much you love Jesus if you do not love his church. Do not tell me how much you love Jesus if you do not love the lost. Paul said, "You are my reason for living." And, "we can bear anything as long as we know that you remain strong in him" (3:8).

PRAISE

"For what thanks can we render to God again for you, for all the joy wherewith we joy for your sakes before our God" (3:9, KJV).

He is saying, "Lord, I can never praise you enough for what you are doing. You have given us people to witness to and they have received Christ. They have grown and matured in the faith. My heart is so excited and so full."

Praise is never based upon man's resources, but always upon God's. Paul was acknowledging here that the work in Thessalonica was the work of God, not the work of man. Man is incapable of doing spiritual work. The basis of praise is not what man has done, but what God has accomplished.

Praise is thanking God. When we give ourselves to God for a lost world, we will have a joy that is abounding, that knows no end. Then we will be praising God continually.

One may say, "You do not understand my problems." It does not matter. Thank God for them. There are things we do not understand. They hurt. But we can say, "Lord, I thank you, even though I do not understand, even though the pain is intense and the pressure is great. Thank you, God, for I have a promise from your Word that all things work together for good, and I will not accuse you of letting anything come into my life that you will not use for good." If we are not thankful to God for everything, then we are accusing God of allowing circumstances that he cannot turn around and make good. Praise God for everything he has done.

PRAYER

"Night and day praying exceedingly that we might see your face, and might perfect that which is lacking in your faith" (3:10, KJV).

In 2:9 Paul said he labored night and day, building tents so he could provide for himself. That way no one in Thessalonica could say that he came to town to see what he could get from others. He worked night and day, but still had time to pray night and day. Prayer was more of a need for him than rest or nourishment.

It is no wonder we do not have the spiritual victories that we desire. It is because of the lack of prayer. We have no sense of urgency in prayer.

The word for "praying" is not the usual word for this in the New Testament. It means to need something, to lack something, to long for something. He is saying, "I need you." Here is that bond again. "By night and by day I longed for you. I longed to God for you."

The word "exceedingly" is an adverb found rarely in the New Testament. It means "fervently." "I longed for you with all my strength. I prayed for you fervently, enthusiastically, zealously." It would make a great difference in our fellowship if we prayed like that.

He prayed that he might help them and supply that which was lacking in their faith. They had some deficiencies, some doctrinal problems. They did not understand the doctrine of the second coming. There were some who had withdrawn and wavered in their faith. There was a good report, but there were still needs in their lives. We never reach the place where we can say, "We have made it." Paul said to the Christians in Philippi, "No, dear brothers, I am still not all I should be but I am bringing all my energies to bear on this one thing: Forgetting the past and looking forward to what lies ahead, I strain to reach the end of the race and receive the prize for which God is calling us up to heaven because of what Christ Jesus did for us" (Phil. 3:13, 14). So he prays for their continued growth and maturity in Christ.

The word "perfect" is a word which means "to knit together, to complete, to cause to be made a unit, a whole." He prays that he might bring to full realization and completeness that which was lacking in their lives, and thus encourage them in their faith.

He is speaking of their faith in God, their trust in him, but also of their doctrinal stance. He longs to strengthen their knowledge of the truth of God.

The thing that stands out so clearly here is the tremendous burden of praying for them. Oh, that we could pray for each other like that! We will never know from how much sin we have been saved and how much temptation we have conquered because someone else prayed for us. We must pray for each other, thus placing the shield of the Holy Spirit around others. There are numerous instances in the New Testament where people were healed, not because they believed, but because someone else believed for them and prayed for them. Let us intercede for each other, lifting each other up, praying for God's power in a person's life, for God's protection over them. God can guide and direct them. I believe God called me to preach because my father and mother prayed for me year after year until God was able to do in my life what he wanted done. Praying by night and by day for each other is a glorious goal for the church fellowship.

Abounding in Love
First Thessalonians 3:11-13

"May God our Father himself and our Lord Jesus send us back to you again. And may the Lord make your love to grow and overflow to each other and to everyone else, just as our love does toward you. This will result in your hearts being made strong, sinless and holy by God our Father, so that you may stand before him guiltless on that day when our Lord Jesus Christ returns with all those who belong to him" (3:11-13).

We are again confronted with a recurring theme that runs throughout Thessalonians: the nature of Christian fellowship, our love and concern for each other. There is, however, a new twist here. All of us know that we should do better than we do. All of us know that we ought to be more loving, more patient, more understanding than we are. We all know that our lives ought to be more like Christ's and we should be looking more toward the coming of the Lord. But in these verses God tells us how we are to do this. He gives us the source of it all.

The thing that jumps out at us is the fact that if any of these things are to be present in our lives, God has to do it. It is not through our resources that we are to love.

Abounding in Love

It is not in our strength that we are to live. It is not by our determination that we are to look toward the second coming of Christ. It is God's power and God's strength in us. It all depends on him.

Paul declares that if he is to come to them again, God will have to make it possible (3:11). God will have to remove obstacles and open the way.

He further states that if they are to love each other, if they are to love all people, God will have to love through them (3:12). Only the working of God's Spirit through them can enable them to so love.

Paul concludes by revealing that they will be accepted by the Lord at his second coming only because of God. It all depends on him. The great apostle reminds us in these verses of our utter and absolute dependence upon God. Often we waste our energies and strength trying to do what only God can do.

Verse 11 has a plural subject and a singular verb. "May God our Father himself and our Lord Jesus send us back." Paul is not giving a theological discussion of the Trinity as such. This is a natural expression of his understanding of the eternal truth that God and Christ are one and the same. We cannot emphasize the deity of Jesus Christ enough.

If someone claims to be a Christian and yet does not believe in the deity of Jesus Christ, he is deceiving others and himself. The deity of Christ is absolutely pivotal in our understanding of Christian truth. It is at the heart of our relationship to God.

The Gnostics of the first century were opposed greatly

by John the Apostle at the point of their unbelief in the deity of Jesus Christ. He declared they could not be of God if they denied the deity of Christ (1 John 2:22, 23).

Paul is emphasizing the reality of the deity of Jesus Christ. He is not *a* way to God; he is *the* way to God. He is not one *like* God; he *is* God. He is not one created by God; he was "with God in the beginning." "By him and for him" were all things created. God and Jesus are one and the same.

Notice the personal pronouns—"our Father," "our Lord Jesus Christ." By faith, the Apostle Paul and these Thessalonian Christians had come into the family of God. Before we can pray to God, there has to be a personal encounter with him. If we are to pray to him in confidence, sure of his provisions and concern for us as his children, there has to be an experience of salvation by which we are born into the family of God. He is our God and our Father.

America today needs a personal God. It is not a question of "Do you believe in God?" but rather, "Is he *your* God?" We must know him and walk with him. He must be both Lord and life to us.

GOD'S PRACTICAL PROVISION

"May God our Father himself and our Lord Jesus send us back to you again" (3:11). The word "send" means "to make straight or to make level." The idea is to prepare a road so that one can travel on it, to open up the way. Paul is saying that even in the very practical matter of taking a journey and visiting friends, God is the One who makes it possible.

The Apostle Paul learned to be dependent on God in the daily affairs of life. I wish we could learn that everything about our lives is significant to God. He cares about our daily experiences, the little frustrations, the little problems, and the little victories. God's provision is always practical. Nothing is too little to talk to God about.

When we realize that God is involved in everything we do, it will really make life exciting. God should be directing the work and preparing the way. If we had the mind of God about every purchase we made, about every word that we spoke, about every relationship we enjoy, it would protect us at many points day by day in our lives.

Unfortunately we only come to God about the great crises and emergencies. Everybody prays when the roof falls in, but what Paul is talking about here is walking with God every day of life. God is interested in the classes we take at school, how we study for them, how we turn in our reports, how we take our tests. He is interested in whom we date, our close friends, how we are doing at work, our relationships with our families, how we spend our leisure time—everything day by day in our lives. God wants us to have the very best possible life.

We are never out of God's care, never away from his concern. As we include him in our daily affairs, he will be there in the crises and emergencies because he is already walking beside us, filling us and providing for us. As

FIRST THESSALONIANS 3:11-13

we practice the presence of God, the big things will take care of themselves.

In fact, we might discover there are no emergencies, because when we walk with the Lord the problems that come along do not seem nearly so big. We are prepared for them because God is there with us. The crises never surprise God.

GOD'S SPIRITUAL PROVISION

"And may the Lord make your love to grow and overflow to each other and to everyone else, just as our love does toward you" (3:12). We do not have to struggle to love each other. God has made spiritual provision for the kind of attitude that ought to exist between us. That simply means that when we do not have the right kind of attitude toward each other, when there is hostility or resentment, God is not in control of our lives. When he is in control, he will make our love *"grow* and *overflow."* Those two words carry a single idea—abundant overflow. God is saying, "I will cause you to have an overflowing love. It will be like water that builds up behind a dam until it reaches the top and then spills over on all of the countryside around. I will give you an overflowing love that spills over to everyone."

Do you know that if we do not love our Christian brethren, we cannot love the lost? If we do not love each other, we will not have a burden for seeing people saved.

This love "will result in your hearts being made strong,

sinless and holy by God our Father, so that you may stand before him guiltless on that day when our Lord Jesus Christ returns with all those who belong to him" (3:13). Our Lord's approval at his second coming depends on how we love each other. We can never have the hand of God in joy and blessing upon our lives if we do not abound in love one for another.

This is not natural to us. We are resentful, jealous, cliquish. It is not easy to love everyone. We all have a problem at this point. But God has made spiritual provision for us so we can love one another and all men. We are to let God teach us how to love.

GOD'S ETERNAL PROVISION
"This will result in your hearts being made strong, sinless and holy by God our Father, so that you may stand before him guiltless on that day when our Lord Jesus Christ returns with all those who belong to him" (3:13). God is giving us an overflowing love to make us strong. "Being made strong" means "to build a foundation, to support, to strengthen, to encourage." God is going to undergird our faith and our relationship with him. God establishes us. God builds the foundation for us to be received by Christ when he comes. It is God's grace that brings fulfillment into our lives and will ultimately carry us into the presence of a returning, reigning Lord Jesus.

How is God going to present us? We will be "sinless." That simply refers to a high quality of living. God did not intend his children to live in the gutter. The Apostle Paul used this word in Philippians 3:6 when he said that he was a Pharisee before he was saved and according to the Law he was "blameless" (KJV). The devoted Jew who lived under the Law and the threat of the judgment of God had a high quality of life. Surely the grace of God will produce nothing less. There should be something different about Christian people. The things we do, the way we act should be uniquely Christian.

We will be "sinless and holy." "Holy" means "set apart for God." It is the same root word translated "saints" (KJV) at the end of the verse. Saints are those who have been set apart for God's purposes and who belong to him. We are his holy ones.

We cannot be like that in ourselves. We naturally do the wrong things. But God has begun an eternal work in us. When we were saved, God did not walk off and leave us. He planted his Spirit deep within us; he planted himself within us. He is able to preserve us sinless and holy. He is able to keep us set apart.

We often live below our privilege. We often compromise and bring things into our lives that we know are not pleasing to God. We must claim God's eternal provision and allow him the liberty to do his work in our lives.

Every chapter in First and Second Thessalonians ends with a reminder of the second coming of Christ. The Lord is coming again. He will return. History is moving toward a climax, when Jesus Christ will return in glory and establish his kingdom. Then we will be presented by God to him, not in our own strength and ingenuity, not in our abilities, but in the power of God who has set us apart for himself.

12
The Will of God
First Thessalonians 4:1-6

"Let me add this, dear brothers: You already know how to please God in your daily living, for you know the commands we gave you from the Lord Jesus himself. Now we beg you—yes, we demand of you in the name of the Lord Jesus—that you live more and more closely to that ideal. For God wants you to be holy and pure, and to keep clear of all sexual sin so that each of you will marry in holiness and honor—not in lustful passion as the heathen do, in their ignorance of God and his ways. And this also is God's will: that you never cheat in this matter by taking another man's wife, because the Lord will punish you terribly for this, as we have solemnly told you before" (4:1-6).

In verses 1 and 2 Paul urges the Thessalonians with all the power in his being to maintain a strong Christian ideal. "We beseech and exhort you" (KJV). These words really mean, "It is urgent and imperative for you to do what we demand." He is not assuming a superior position and preaching down to them. He is saying very simply, "God has given me a message for you. Hear it as from the Lord."

The Will of God

He calls them "dear brothers." He identifies with them. They were together in this thing. It was a word from God to all of them, Paul included.

A BINDING REQUIREMENT

"You already know how to please God in your daily living, for you know the commands we gave you from the Lord Jesus himself" (4:1). The KJV renders this, "ye ought to walk and to please God." The word "ought" is often translated "must" in the New Testament. Jesus used this word when he said to Nicodemus, "You must be born again." There is force in this word. Here is something binding, something we must do.

Christian service is not an option for the Christian. When we gave our hearts to Jesus Christ, we received the free grace of God that brings forgiveness and salvation. However, whether or not we will serve God is not up to us. God requires it. Christian service is not just reserved for a few super-saints who happen to like that kind of thing. It is for everybody. It is what it means to be a Christian. We have preached free grace so long that we have developed a cheap discipleship. Beware of thinking you can receive the free grace of God and ignore God for the rest of your life. If we belong to Jesus Christ, then we *belong* to Jesus Christ! He owns us. We are his slaves. Therefore, we must glorify God in body and soul, which are his. We must please God.

Many Christians are miserable because they don't seek

to serve and please God every day. Christianity is more than just a "Sunday-morning-go-to-church" thing! It is a way in which we live, the way we dress, the way we act, the way we talk. Show me someone who is miserable as a Christian and I will show you a person who does not live in the awareness that he belongs to God.

We must be honest with ourselves. Do we want to please God more than anything (or anyone) else? We will never be happy if God is not happy with us. But he has made provision for us to please him.

Paul continues, "so ye would abound more and more" (KJV). God wants us to do more than just exist. He wants us to possess abundant life. Many people think, "If I get serious with God, he will take all the fun out of life." No, he will put zest into life! Real monotony and drudgery is to go on a rat race of one sensation after another, always coming up empty, frustrated, and guilty. But when we come to God, he puts adventure and excitement into our lives. He puts peace and fulfillment in our hearts.

Jesus said, "The thief's purpose is to steal, kill and destroy. My purpose is to give life in all its fullness" (John 10:10). God wants us to really live.

Life is complicated to many people. They are always looking for ulterior motives, always disturbed, always finding something of a problem. But life is simple when we realize that we are not our own. We have become God's problem. Whatever worries we have are his problems. When we give our problems to him, he takes the burden and gives us the victory. We cannot beat a deal like that! That is what being a Christian means.

The Will of God

A BEAUTIFUL REVELATION

"For ye know what commandments we gave you by the Lord Jesus" (4:2, KJV). The word "commandments" is a military term used when a commanding officer gives orders to the troops in the field. The commanding officer orders, "This is what you are to do." The soldiers reply, "Yes, sir." The Apostle Paul was saying, "We gave you orders from God, our Commanding General." When we let God direct our lives, he will assume the responsibility for them.

"For this is the will of God, even your sanctification" (4:3, KJV). God has a will, a plan, for our lives. Our lives are not subject to chance. Our lives are not simply the results of what may happen to us. Here is the beautiful revelation that God cares for us enough to plan our lives. He has a wonderful purpose for our lives.

The God of the vastness of space is also the God of minute detail. The God of the telescope is the God of the microscope. The God who loves the whole world loves me individually. He has a purpose for all creation and nature, and he has a plan and a purpose for my life. He cares about whom I marry, where I work, where I attend church, how I use my money, how I spend my time. He has an interest in everything in my life.

In the original language the definite article is not present here. It does not say, "for this is *the* will of God," but simply, "This is will of God." The reason for this is that he is not telling us everything that is involved in the will of God in this passage. God also wills that we pray, that we be a witness, that we be faithful in the use of our possessions, etc. Here we see purity as the will of God.

Many people are paranoid about the will of God. But if we will do what he tells us plainly to do, we will not have any trouble deciding things that may not be so clearly spelled out in the Scripture.

"This is the will of God, even your sanctification" (4:3, KJV). There are three New Testament words that theologians toss around. Justification refers to salvation. Sanctification involves living the Christian life, progressing toward the goal of maturity, and becoming like Jesus. Glorification anticipates our final state when God will take us home to be with him and we will be like him.

When we come to Christ and get saved, God is not through with us. That is not the end. We are to grow into the likeness of Christ. We are to have direction for our daily lives. We are to have the mind of Christ in us. Sanctification is the name given to the process of growth from salvation to the grave, or to the coming of Christ.

If you do not like me now, just wait. God is not through! He is changing me each day. The Christian life is a process of growth toward maturity. It is a process of progress toward holiness. It is a matter of growing to be like Jesus. God leads us by his Spirit toward maturity in Christ.

A BODILY REALITY
"This is the will of God, even your sanctification, that ye should abstain from fornication: that every one of you should know how to possess his vessel in sanctification and honor; not in the lust of concupiscence, even as the

The Will of God

Gentiles, which know not God" (4:3, 4, KJV). "Concupiscence" literally means "the passion of lust."

God's will and purpose is expressed by our bodies. In another place, Paul says, "And so, dear brothers, I plead with you to give your bodies to God" (Rom. 12:1). When we are saved, God not only buys and purchases our souls and minds, but our bodies. For this reason, any moral abuse of our bodies is outside the will of God. It may seem strange that the Apostle Paul would talk to young Christians about sexual immorality. But we must understand that in Thessalonica pagan worship was prominent. Part of the pagan worship was sexual immorality by and with religious prostitutes who were used for "religious" purposes.

In the first 500 years of the Roman Empire divorce was virtually unknown. By the time Paul wrote this letter, divorce was common, so much so that one of the philosophers said, "Women are married to be divorced and divorced to be married." It was a promiscuous society, condoning immorality and unfaithfulness. It mocked the home and the sanctity of the marriage relationship. It would be easy for these young Christians to be drawn back into the immorality of their society.

Today there are more divorce petitions filed than marriage licenses. When we combine with that the multiplied thousands who engage in premarital and extramarital sex, we realize that Paul's admonition is much needed now. Everything that the New Testament tells us about our bodies is based on the fact that our bodies belong to God. That is why we cannot abuse them. God says, "That body is mine."

Specifically, he is talking here about immorality. He says, "Keep clear of all sexual sin." This refers to immorality of any kind. The Greek word here is *pornea*. We get our word "pornography" from it. It is used both in the New Testament and the Greek classics as an expression of any sexual impurity, any sexual misuse of our bodies. This would include homosexuality and the promiscuous use of our bodies prior to marriage as well as the adulterous use of our bodies beyond marriage. If we are married, there is one person with whom we are to gain sexual gratification and no one else. If we are not married, God will give us grace to keep ourselves sexually pure. That is what Paul is saying.

What is God's alternative to sex sin? "So that each of you will marry in holiness and honor."

Listen to what the Apostle Paul declares to the church at Corinth: "Now the body is not for fornication, but for the Lord; and the Lord for the body" (1 Cor. 6:13, KJV). And, "Know ye not that your bodies are the members of Christ? Shall I then take the members of Christ, and make them the members of a harlot? God forbid. What! know ye not that he which is joined to a harlot is one body? for two, saith he, shall be one flesh. But he that is joined unto the Lord is one spirit. Flee fornication. Every sin that a man doeth is without the body; but he that committeth fornication sinneth against his own body" (1 Cor. 6:15-18, KJV). We think we are satisfying the body, but every time we engage in immorality we are killing the body, sinning against it. It is out of that context that Paul says, "Your body is the temple of the Holy Ghost which is in you . . . ye are not your own. For ye are bought with a price: therefore glorify God in your body, and in your spirit, which are God's" (1 Cor. 6:19, 20, KJV).

In Romans, Paul says, "Do not let sin control your puny body any longer" (Rom. 6:12). The two words "lust" and "concupiscence" (4:5, KJV) refer to unbridled lust and passion. They describe someone who cannot control his sexual appetite, who is completely dominated and controlled by it. That is the way the heathen act. God's people must be different.

"And this also is God's will: that you never cheat in this matter by taking another man's wife, because the Lord will punish you terribly for this, as we have solemnly told you before" (4:6). A person who commits sexual impurity greatly hurts another as well as himself. When we violate this commandment, God will punish us. That does not mean that God is going to strike out in revenge to get back at us. It means that God will make sure that when we violate his laws we face the consequences.

Paul says, "We have solemnly told you before." That law is as absolute as the law of gravity. There will never be a day when we can violate the laws of purity relating to our bodies and not suffer the consequences.

Interestingly, the word *pornea* is also used in the Bible in relation to God. We are told not to "fornicate" against God. That means that when we worship anything less than God Almighty, we are spiritually immoral. We have violated the purity of God. Thus, we all stand condemned, for either in our spirits as we worship other things than God and his Son Jesus Christ, or by our bodies, as we use them for immoral activities, we have violated this law.

But there is good news! Our sins can be forgiven. God can give us a fresh start. We can be cleansed and forgiven.

God has a beautiful plan and purpose for our lives, even our sanctification, our growing to be like him. We will never know happiness until we respond to God and to his plan for our lives.

Called unto Holiness
First Thessalonians 4:7-12

"For God has not called us to be dirty-minded and full of lust, but to be holy and clean. If anyone refuses to live by these rules he is not disobeying the rules of men but of God who gives his Holy Spirit to you. But concerning the pure brotherly love that there should be among God's people, I don't need to say very much, I'm sure! For God himself is teaching you to love one another. Indeed, your love is already strong toward all the Christian brothers throughout your whole nation. Even so, dear friends, we beg you to love them more and more. This should be your ambition: to live a quiet life, minding your own business and doing your own work, just as we told you before. As a result, people who are not Christians will trust and respect you, and you will not need to depend on others for enough money to pay your bills" (4:7-12).

THE PURPOSE
"For" or "therefore" always looks back to what has been said. Because of all that has been said, "God has not

called us to be dirty-minded and full of lust." God has not called us to be evil and impure, but to be pure and holy. Any impure use of our bodies, any immorality is a violation of the basic purpose for which God has called us.

God called us for the purpose of holiness and purity. He has called us to have that quality of holiness that he himself enjoys—the quality of rightness of character, of the right use of all that we have.

THE PRESENCE
"If anyone refuses to live by these rules he is not disobeying the rules of men, but of God who gives his Holy Spirit to you" (4:8). The word "refuses" could be translated as "rejects, disregards, counts the commandments as nothing, as though they are of no consequence, no significance." Such a person does not feel bound by them. If we count the words of God as nothing, we are not despising man, but God.

Immorality is a sin against God, because God the Spirit lives within the Christian. Immorality is an attack against God. It is to declare to God, "I do not care about you. I will not be bound by what you have said. I will not pay any attention to your commandments." Thus we reject the counsel of God and the Spirit of God.

"God... gives his Holy Spirit to you." "Gives" is in the present tense in the Greek, meaning that God is continuously giving his Spirit to his children. When we use our bodies as objects of impurity rather than holiness, we are not simply sinning against a God who at

FIRST THESSALONIANS 4:7-12

some point in the past gave us his Spirit, but we are in reality shaking our fists in the face of a God who is right now giving us his Spirit.

Sometimes we wonder why our lives have been filled with confusion and despair. When we rebel against God, we are shaking our fists in the face of a God who is right now doing his work in our lives, and we reap the tragic consequences. We cannot sin and get away with it. His Spirit will not allow it.

THE PASSION

"But concerning the pure brotherly love that there should be among God's people, I don't need to say very much, I'm sure! For God himself is teaching you to love one another. Indeed, your love is already strong toward all the Christian brothers throughout your whole nation. Even so, dear friends, we beg you to love them more and more" (4:9, 10). Our love for each other should be zealous, enthusiastic, passionate, and compassionate.

Paul commends the Thessalonians by saying that they are practicing this. God has given us a love for each other. But at the same time, "Even so, dear friends, we beg you to love them more and more." In this life we never arrive. We can never rest on our laurels. We can never get careless about the relationships that we have. We need to work at our love for each other.

The proper kind of love doesn't just happen. It must be cultivated. Just as we were warned in earlier verses not to cheat in marriage by being impure, so we must not cheat each other in the fellowship of the church by refusing to love each other in the Lord. Brotherly love must be a passion in our lives. It must be a reality in the life of the church. We must all love each other and care about each other, lifting each other up and serving God in that way.

"Love them more and more." Work at it. Be thoughtful of each other. Care about each other. Express kindness toward each other. Be gracious toward each other. Lift each other up. Pray for each other. Visit each other. Be a part of brotherly love and mutual sharing.

Here again the word "love" is *agape*, a self-giving, self-denying love, a love that keeps on loving even if it is not reciprocated.

The one really distinguishing characteristic of our Christian fellowship ought to be our love. We will not find the kind of love that draws hearts to God anywhere else but in the church. I pray that God would press upon our hearts the need of kindness and encouragement to each other so that we might abound more and more in brotherly love.

THE PURSUIT
"And that ye study to be quiet, and to do your own business, and to work with your own hands, as we commanded you; that ye may walk honestly toward them that are without, and that ye may have lack of nothing" (4:11, 12, KJV). The word "study" means "to strive earnestly for, to be ambitious." Someone who is ambi-

tious devotes much energy toward reaching a particular goal. Paul declares that we should strive to be quiet.

The word "quiet" is a word which means tranquillity. We are to seek to have peace in our hearts and souls. We must give ourselves to a pursuit that will allow God to bring his tranquillity and peace into our lives.

We may not be enjoying God's peace, but he wants us to. Our hearts may be distressed, but God does not want it to be that way. We cannot blame anyone but ourselves if we are miserable today. No one has to live in despair; we can let God's peace control our hearts.

Paul also tells them to "mind their own business." This is the first indication we have that some of them had gotten lazy. Apparently when they heard the wonderful truth about the second coming of Jesus Christ, some of them decided to rejoice in his return, then quit their jobs and refused to work. To make matters worse, they demanded that the rich people of the church take care of them. That is why Paul says, "He who does not work shall not eat" (2 Thess. 3:10). God's kingdom has no place for laziness. It is not a Christian virtue. "Work with your own hands" (4:11, KJV). We must do what God has given us to do.

This has several applications. God gave to the church pastors and deacons, spiritual leadership. We are to pray and support those God has given to us to lead us. As we give attention to the work God has assigned to each of us, we fulfill God's purpose for ourselves individually and for the church collectively.

It is amazing that the people who are the most unhappy about the way the church conducts business are usually the people who are the most unhappy in their lives. God tells us to give attention to what our own responsibilities are; he will take care of his. We are not to meddle in someone else's work or affairs, but do what God has given us to do.

If we all obey God in our specific assignments, then the body can move properly. My hand does not tell my head what to do. If it tries, I am in trouble. Every member of the church has a clear responsibility, and must perform it for the spiritual welfare of the entire church.

"Work with your own hands" (4:11, KJV). Christianity dignifies labor and leaves no place for laziness. Most of the people in the early church were laborers, literally working with their hands. Christianity has always been the champion of the common people. When we work hard we will "have lack of nothing" (4:12, KJV). We will have enough to purchase everything we need for our families.

The Christian is not supposed to be a parasite. We are to work hard and not sit around expecting someone else to take care of us. The same thing could be said of spiritual things, too. There are many spiritual sponges, people who sit around wanting people to spoon-feed them. We can't expect the church to make us mature if we don't discipline ourselves enough to spend time with God in our homes. If all the Bible we ever get is what we hear from the pulpit, we will be weak and frustrated.

"You have been Christians a long time now, and you ought to be teaching others, but instead you have dropped back to the place where you need someone to teach you all over again the very first principles in God's

Word. You are like babies who can drink only milk, not old enough for solid food. And when a person is still living on milk it shows he isn't very far along in the Christian life, and doesn't know much about the difference between right and wrong. He is still a baby-Christian!" (Heb. 5:12, 13). God wants us to grow up and be mature. We are not to be spiritual parasites.

14
The Coming of the Lord
First Thessalonians 4:13-18

The Apostle Paul begins this section, "I want you to know" ("I would not have you to be ignorant," KJV). He concludes, "So comfort and encourage each other with this news." He is reminding us that ignorance of biblical and eternal truths bring a lack of comfort. What we do not know will hurt us. Most of the time when we as children of God are distressed and distraught it is because of spiritual ignorance, a lack of understanding of spiritual truths. We need to know what God has said if we are to live in peace, if we are to live with an awareness that God is in control and that history is moving toward a victorious climax.

The Apostle Paul had been with the Thessalonians for perhaps a few weeks, a few months at best. He taught them about the second coming of Christ, but did not have the opportunity to give them a complete and exhaustive study. Some of the people had died since Paul had left. Those remaining were concerned that all of the glory and excitement concerning Christ's coming again would be missed by those who had died. What would happen to them?

The early church shared in a close-knit fellowship, in a

*The Coming
of the Lord*

deep bond of love. They really cared for each other. Those who were alive did not want those who had passed on to miss anything. They did not want them to be cheated out of any good thing that God had for those who were alive. Thus, responding to their love and concern, the Apostle Paul writes to tell them about believers who had passed on and about what would happen to them at the coming of the Lord. A love and a fellowship such as they shared created a concern that even death could not break.

We who so often have little concern for each other need to be reminded often of the depths of Christian love. Just as we are never separated from the love of Christ (Rom. 8:38, 39), there is nothing that should tear us apart from our brethren in Christ Jesus.

THE CONTRAST
"I want you to know what happens to a Christian when he dies so that when it happens, you will not be full of sorrow, as those are who have no hope" (4:13). Those in the world had no hope at all. They had no anticipation of ever seeing departed loved ones again. Death had left them in despair. They saw no hope of life beyond the grave. Granted, some of the ancient philosophers and pagan religions hinted at life after death. The Stoics said there may be a conditional experience beyond the grave. But they fell short of confident anticipation. The Epicurean philosophers of Greece, who patterned the thought

and set the philosophical stage in the ancient world, said that when one died he stopped existing.

In contrast, the Apostle Paul declared, "O death, where then your victory? Where then your sting? For sin—the sting that causes death—will all be gone; and the law, which reveals our sins, will no longer be our judge. How we thank God for all of this! It is he who makes us victorious through Jesus Christ our Lord!" (1 Cor. 15:55-57). Apart from Jesus Christ there is no hope beyond the grave, but with him there is eternal life.

Paul was saying, "I want you, in contrast to a helpless world, not to sorrow as though you had no hope." He did not say that they should not grieve, but not to sorrow as though there were no hope. We are not to grieve like those who are outside the cause of Christ.

Notice he says, "concerning them which are asleep" (4:13, KJV) and then, "Jesus died" (4:14, KJV). For the Christians he said, they "are asleep." For Jesus he declared that he "died." Why the difference? In the New Testament there are two views of death. For some, death is a natural experience at the end of life, a transition through which an individual goes into the eternal presence of God. For others, death is a horrible experience, the result of sin and the fruit of rebellion, a thing to be feared and dreaded.

Concerning Jesus, Paul used the word for that dreaded form of death. Jesus died. He was dead, not asleep. He bore the agony of death, the consequences of sin, our sin. Jesus Christ experienced all of the horror of death. But for us, the horror has been taken out of it. For us, the anguish has been removed. For us, it is described as if we were simply going to sleep.

This does not refer to a soul-sleep or intermediate state. It is simply showing that just as we cast ourselves confidently into the arms of sleep when we are tired, so we who are in Christ can face death in confidence and peace. Jesus died, but we sleep. He died so that we can pass through death's door to be with him.

This picture of sleep shows us the confidence and the lack of fear that accompany the Christian's attitude toward death. Also, when we wake up in the morning, we wake up to a new day. For the child of God, a new day dawns at the grave. God's children awake to a new world of eternal life, eternal delight, and eternal joy in and with Jesus Christ.

"Concerning them which are asleep, that ye sorrow not, even as others which have no hope" (4:13, KJV). The philosophy of the world is, "Live it up, for death will come and that will be the end." Rather than fearing death and frantically rushing through life, the child of God views life and death in the context of what Jesus Christ has done. What a hope there is for us in Jesus Christ!

THE CONCLUSION
"For since we believe that Jesus died and then came back to life again, we can also believe that when Jesus returns, God will bring back with him all the Christians who have died" (4:14).

The phrase, "We believe," is a conditional phrase but does not convey uncertainty. It speaks as though the condition were already fulfilled. Since we believe that Jesus died and bore for us the agony, the anguish, and the horror of death, and that he conquered death by rising victoriously, we know that God will not forget those who sleep in Jesus. Our Lord will bring them with him when he comes.

This phrase, "sleep in Jesus" (KJV), has a hidden delight. Probably it should be translated "sleep through Jesus," as the preposition there in the original language is more often translated "through." The idea is that those who die, die through Jesus. They are never separated from him. He is the being that gives them life, and he is the one who takes them through the experience of death. Thus, those believers who have died cannot be separated from God by death. Those who have passed on, who have faced death through Jesus Christ, will be brought back with the Lord.

THE COMING

"I can tell you this directly from the Lord" (4:15). Jesus may have spoken this during his ministry and it is recorded here rather than in the Gospels, or it might simply be a revelation straight from God. Whichever, it is clear that this is an eternal truth spoken by the Lord Jesus Christ himself.

"I can tell you this directly from the Lord: that we who are still living when the Lord returns will not rise to meet him ahead of those who are in their graves." That phrase "we who are still living" has been taken by some to mean that the Apostle Paul expected to be alive himself at the time of the second coming of Christ. It may mean that, but the structure in the original language does not confirm that. What he is simply saying is that those who are alive when the Lord comes will not have an advantage over those who have died. Those who have died will not be in a position of inferiority, but will rise first. The living will not precede the dead.

"For the Lord himself will come down from heaven with a mighty shout and with the soul-stirring cry of the archangel and the great trumpet-call of God. And the believers who are dead will be the first to rise to meet the Lord" (4:16). "The Lord himself." When God calls the age to an end, when the trumpet of God sounds and the message rings to the four corners of the world for God's people to assemble at the feet of Jesus, when the time comes for us to be joined perfectly, completely, and wholly with him for all eternity, it is going to be Jesus himself who sounds that call. No angel or other created being will carry that message. The Lord himself shall come.

When he comes, the Lord himself will give the resurrection command. All who have died through Jesus Christ will hear our Lord and will rise to meet the Lord in the air.

The trumpet of God was used throughout the Old Testament as a signal for deliverance. When Moses was on the Mount, God's trumpet sounded loudly (Ex. 19:16). The prophets Zephaniah and Zechariah spoke of the trumpet being sounded and in the sounding of the trumpet God's deliverance came (Zeph. 1:16; Zech. 9:14). The trumpet announced that deliverance had come.

Paul declared, "For there will be a trumpet blast from the sky and all the Christians who have died will suddenly come alive" (1 Cor. 15:52). The archangel of God will sound the trumpet and herald deliverance. Those Christians who are still alive will be delivered from it all. They will be given glorified bodies, no more to be assaulted by Satan. Those who have died, whose spirits have been separated from their bodies, shall be reunited with their bodies. They will possess the perfect union of body and spirit with an eternal God.

We shall be caught up in the clouds to meet the Lord in the air and so ever remain with the Lord. This refers to the rapture of the church, the time when we are caught up, when we are taken up to be with the Lord.

Satan is called "the prince of the power of the air." The air, the atmosphere surrounding the earth, is the domain of Satan and his demons. Yet, when the Lord returns we are going to meet him in the air, on Satan's home ground. This will demonstrate conclusively and without any question the total victory and domination of Jesus Christ over the forces of evil. No more shall Satan rule, for the Lord of lords and King of kings will have come and we will have been raised to be kings and princes with him. In Satan's own territory we shall meet the Lord.

A great reunion will then take place. Paul says, "Caught up with them" (4:17). We shall rise with the departed saints who preceded us in death. This is a very strong testimony to the reunion that is ours in Jesus

Christ. Have we lost loved ones? We will be together again. We will know them again. We will worship with them again. We will serve God with them again. We are going to be raised up to meet the Lord with those who have gone before, and so shall we ever be with the Lord in wonderful fellowship.

We are going to meet the Lord. The word "meet" (4:16) is a word which means "to welcome a great person." It refers to preparation to meet a great dignitary. We are going to meet the Lord, the King of kings, the Lord of lords. We would not carelessly enter into the presence of a king. We would prepare for it. Jesus said, "Blessed is that servant, whom his lord when he cometh shall find so doing" (Matt. 24:46, KJV).

When Jesus comes and we are caught up to be with him, there will never be another invitation extended to those on the earth who are alive at that time. His coming will seal the fate of all. Either they will have been for Christ or against him. They will never have another opportunity. Should our Lord come today for his people, the door would be closed forever.

THE COMFORT
"So comfort and encourage each other with this news" (4:18). There is such tenderness here. The Thessalonian believers loved each other. When one hurt, they all hurt. When one suffered, they all suffered. When one grieved, they all grieved. So Paul could say to them, "Listen to

what I declare and share it. Comfort each other and thus deepen your love."

We have great need to comfort each other. Is there a husband who is gone from your presence? Has life been less than full since he left? You will meet him in the air when Jesus comes. Is there a wife whose absence has made life sad? Take heart, for Jesus is going to come and you will meet her in the air. Is there a parent, son, daughter, brother, or sister whom you have laid in the cold earth of this planet? Take heart! Be comforted by this, for they are not lost and forgotten. They are real persons; they are with the Lord. When he comes again, they shall rise first.

Do you stand and look death in the face? Has the doctor said, "You have cancer. You have a heart condition. You have a few weeks, months, or years to live at best"? Take heart. Death is not a horror for God's children. It is a delight to face death through Jesus Christ.

The days of this earth are brief. Eternity is unending. Do you look into the face of a loved one who, unless a miracle of God intervenes, will pass through the valley of the shadow of death within the next few weeks or months? Do you face the laying aside of one dear to your heart? God has said, "When Jesus comes again, those who have blissfully been rocked into the arms of sleep through Jesus Christ will be raised first."

For those outside of Christ, death will be horror, a hopelessness, a despair. But through Jesus Christ, the very worst that death can do is tear down this old body in which I live and usher me into the very presence of God.

*The Coming
of the Lord*

I shall be with him forever. When Jesus comes, he will not leave me behind. He will bring me with him to meet those I have left behind, and we will meet together with the Lord and there shall never be another good-bye or another tear. We shall forever be with the Lord.

Do not let hopeless despair bring darkness because of the uncertainty of life. Do not be ignorant concerning those who are asleep. Rather, know what God says and then comfort each other in it.

The future is bright. In contrast to the despair of this world, God tells us that not one believer who has died is forgotten. Not one soul who has passed on is lost if he faced death through Jesus Christ. God grant it that every one of us will be so prepared that when that great day shall come and the resurrection command is given and the trumpet of deliverance sounds, every one of us shall rise to be with him.

15

A Thief in the Night
First Thessalonians 5:1-8

"When is all this going to happen? I really don't need to say anything about that, dear brothers, for you know perfectly well that no one knows. That day of the Lord will come unexpectedly like a thief in the night. When people are saying, 'All is well, everything is quiet and peaceful'—then, all of a sudden, disaster will fall upon them as suddenly as a woman's birth pains begin when her child is born. And these people will not be able to get away anywhere—there will be no place to hide. But, dear brothers, you are not in the dark about these things, and you won't be surprised as by a thief when that day of the Lord comes. For you are all children of the light and of the day, and do not belong to darkness and night. So be on your guard, not asleep like the others. Watch for his return and stay sober. Night is the time for sleep and the time when people get drunk. But let us who live in the light keep sober, protected by the armor of faith and love, and wearing as our helmet the happy hope of salvation" (5:1-8).

APPLICATION

Paul has already answered the question about believers who have died and now await the resurrection call. Now he deals with the concern, "When is all this going to happen?" (5:1). There are always questions about when God is coming back again and what it is all going to be like. The disciples, in talking with Jesus, asked, "Lord, wilt thou at this time restore again the kingdom to Israel?" (Acts 1:6, KJV). Jesus replied that these are matters known only to God. Our responsibility is to be ready for Christ's return. It is God's responsibility to work out the time and the details of that coming.

Apparently the same kind of questions were being asked in Thessalonica, and by us today. What are the signs of Christ's coming? Are we near the return of the Lord? Paul declared that the Thessalonians knew everything they needed to know, but were not applying it. Could the same be true of us?

Paul speaks first concerning "the times and the seasons" (KJV). These are two different words in the original language. "Times" is the Greek word from which we get "chronology." It refers to sequence of time, and here the sequence of events accompanying the Lord's return.

"Seasons" is a very difficult word to bring into the English language. Rather than dealing with sequence and quantity of time, such as twenty-four hours in a day or seven days in a week, it speaks about the *quality* of time. It refers to the quality or character of Christ's coming. What more do we need to know? "I really don't need to say anything about that" (5:1).

FIRST THESSALONIANS 5:1-8

The sequence of events surrounding the second coming of Christ becomes a preoccupation with many. Paul is saying here, "You already have been informed about everything you need to know." That ought to be a solemn warning against making too much of the details and chronology of the second coming. The truth is that no man knows the way or time God is going to bring these things to pass. But God has given in his Word clear instructions about our attitude toward his coming.

The Thessalonians (and we) had received enough basic teaching. Now they needed to apply it, live by it, and let it be seen in their lives.

"You know perfectly well" (5:2). They already had knowledge of all they needed to know. Now they needed to put it to work. All of us have a great tendency to seek additional light even though we are not living up to the light we already have. Our problem with the Word of God is not with the passages we do not understand, but with passages we do understand but don't apply. Anyone who does not apply understood teachings of the Word of God to his life is not a growing and maturing Christian. There are many people who would have us believe that they are deeply spiritual people, and yet their lives are in open violation of the Scriptures of God.

We are living in a world that is disregarding God and heading toward cataclysmic destruction. Of all people, Christians ought to be doing what God told them to do. Do not be preoccupied with fascinating speculations or theological guessing games. Apply what you know. Give yourself to the things that God has plainly told you to do.

ARBITRATION

"That day of the Lord will come unexpectedly like a thief in the night. When people are saying, 'All is well, everything is quiet and peaceful'—then, all of a sudden, disaster will fall upon them as suddenly as a woman's birth pains begin when her child is born. And these people will not be able to get away anywhere—there will be no place to hide" (5:2, 3). The day of the Lord was an ancient idea. The prophet Amos spoke centuries before New Testament times concerning it. According to the Old Testament, it was to be a day of judgment, a day when God sets right that which was wrong, a day the lost were to fear though God's people were to welcome it with anticipation and joy.

When the New Testament came along, the same idea of judgment was declared. Peter talked about the day of judgment (2 Peter 2:9). Paul spoke of the day of wrath and the revelation of the judgment of God (Romans 2:5). It is also called "the day of redemption" (KJV), speaking of the deliverance that will come to God's children on that day (Ephesians 4:30). It is called "the day of God" (2 Peter 3:12, KJV), "the day of Jesus Christ" (Philippians 1:6), "the day of the Lord Jesus" (1 Corinthians 5:5, KJV), "the day of our Lord Jesus Christ" (1 Corinthians 1:8, KJV). In 2 Thessalonians 1:10 (KJV), it is simply called "that day." In John 6:39 (KJV) it is called "the last day." Jude 6 (KJV) calls it "the great day."

Whatever else it may be, the day of the Lord is a day of judgment, a day when God moves in judgment to vindicate his people and to punish the wicked. God is saying, "I will take care of things. I will set the record straight.

Victory will come, totally and completely."

This day of the Lord is going to come as a thief in the night; that is, it will be unexpected. No one gets a note from a thief saying, "Tomorrow night I am going to rob your house." If we did, we would be prepared. The Lord Jesus Christ is going to come unexpected by those who are not looking for him. For those who are anticipating his return, he is not coming as a thief, but it will be a surprise to those who are living without any thought of God, eternity, or salvation.

The return of the Lord will come at a time when the unbelievers speak of peace and safety. They will view the situation and conclude that everything is fine. The economy may be on the upswing. There may be peace across the world and everything may look brighter than ever before. But God's children who are watching the signs of the time carefully and who are in fellowship with God will know that the coming of the Lord could be soon. At a time when everything is being promoted as success, with utopia on the way, Jesus will return.

This is why I do not believe the church is going to go through the tribulation. The last half of the tribulation is going to be hell on earth, a terrible time of great tragedy and terror. The Lord is going to come when people are rejoicing in peace and safety, not knowing what lies ahead.

It would be foolish for us to put a baby in the middle of the freeway at rush hour! That is the picture here. Here is the world playing in the midst of great danger, living as if everything was great. All of a sudden great catastrophe and destruction will fall upon them. When men shall cry

"All is well," the wrath of God will come upon them.

"All of a sudden, disaster will fall upon them." The word "sudden" is an adjective very rarely found in the New Testament. It is a word that speaks of complete surprise and great swiftness. Only a blinking of the eye and it is here. Paul said Christ will return "in the twinkling of an eye" (1 Cor. 15:52). The destruction referred to here does not just mean the death of the body, but eternal separation from God.

This will come upon them as "a woman's birth pains ... there will be no place to hide." The point here is that when a woman begins to have labor pains, when the child is ready to be born, it is inevitable that the birth will take place. When the labor pains set in, there is no doubt what will follow.

Those who are not in the family of God will be shut out from the kingdom of God. There will be no additional chance. There will be no escape from the judgment of God.

Many people live as if they have put something over on God, as if God does not know what they are doing. Do not be deceived. You cannot fool God. Whatever one sows, he will reap. The judgment of God will come upon an unbelieving world. Nothing can prevent it.

AFFIRMATION
The lost world is going to be in darkness, unprepared for the Lord's return. None of them will escape. "But,

FIRST THESSALONIANS 5:1-8

dear brothers, you are not in the dark about these things, and you won't be surprised as by a thief when that day of the Lord comes. For you are all children of the light and of the day, and do not belong to darkness and night. So be on your guard, not asleep like the others. Watch for his return and stay sober. Night is the time for sleep and the time when people get drunk. But let us who live in the light keep sober, protected by the armor of faith and love, and wearing as our helmet the happy hope of salvation" (5:4-8). When Jesus comes again for us, it will be natural for us to say, "Praise the Lord. Hallelujah!" It will be no surprise to us, for we are not in darkness.

We are children of light and children of the day. We do not belong to the night or darkness. In Semitic languages, and especially the languages of the Bible, when someone is called a "son of" or "child of" something, it means that characterizes their lives. We are sons of light. Light characterizes our lives.

Our lives have the nature of light. We are not children of sin, darkness, and evil, but of the light. Jesus is the light of the world and we are the light of the world, because we reflect his light. We are to be different from the world. Do not say you are a Christian, yet live like the children of darkness.

God's children do sin, but God has made provision for that (1 John 2:1, 2). Our lives ought to be characterized by godliness.

We are to "be on guard, not asleep like the others." The lost world is sleeping, merrily going its way unaware that judgment is coming. The world does not care anything about Jesus Christ. All the world cares about is prestige, power, and possessions. God help us if that is all we care about.

We are to "watch," the opposite of the word "asleep." Rather than slumbering and ignoring the situation, we are to be alert. The word "watch" is used throughout the New Testament concerning the second coming. The Christian is not only to be awake, but is to be looking for the Lord's return.

It would make a great deal of difference in how we lived if we would wake up daily looking for Jesus to come back. We would exercise daily vigilance, watching and anticipating his return.

We are to "keep sober." Paul is not speaking of abstaining from alcoholic beverages. "Sober" refers to a discipline of life. We are to be in control of our lives. We are not to be sleeping, with our heads in the sand. We are to be alert and watching for the return of Christ, disciplining ourselves in the things that need to be done while the Lord tarries.

Verse 7 reminds us that those in darkness sleep at night, or if they are drunk they are drunk at night. They live in the night of sin and the darkness of rebellion against God, as if there were no need to be concerned. That is their pattern of life.

Rather than living like that, we are to "keep sober, protected by the armor of faith" in God (5:8). Life is a warfare, a battle. Here Paul mentions just two pieces of armor, not the complete list as he did in Ephesians: the helmet and armor or breastplate. The helmet and the breastplate are the first two things that one would put on if he were going into battle. It would be foolish to put on all the other armor but leave either the helmet or breastplate off. These are absolutely vital.

The armor mentioned here is defensive armor, not offensive. Paul does not talk about a spear to attack the enemy, but of putting on the helmet and breastplate. He is dealing with our defense against the lethargy and indifference that can come upon God's children, just as it does the world. He is talking about our defense against the things that would dilute our witness and take away our effectiveness.

There are three things that we absolutely have to have. He mentioned them earlier: faith, hope, and love, the trinity of godly characteristics, the triad of virtue that should be demonstrated in the life of every child of God. All of the other characteristics of the child of God emanate from these.

We cannot separate faith and love. If we have faith, we have love. If we have love, we have faith. They are part of the same package. That is the gift of God for the child of God who is walking in fellowship with him.

None of the characteristics that are produced in the Christian's life are produced by his own strength. It is God who works in and through us. Faith and love are gifts of God to our lives. We are to put on the breastplate of faith and love. The helmet is the hope of salvation, the anticipation of ultimate victory. This is not only freedom from the penalty of sin, but from its very presence and power. That is the hope of salvation.

"Salvation" is a favorite Pauline word. He uses it to remind us of the dreadful consequences of sin. Man needs to be saved. Sin has destroyed man's hope for happiness. There is no way we can have a good marriage, a good job, a good life unless we have salvation from the pressures that sin places upon us.

People are dying. Unless we are caring and compassionate, concerned for the work of God in a dying world, reaching out as children of light, standing firm upon God's Word and living under his control, we are sinning against our calling. We must not live like those in darkness. We must put on the armor of light and be prepared when the day of the Lord comes.

16
Avoiding the Day of Wrath
First Thessalonians 5:9-11

This passage begins with the word "for." Because judgment is coming, because the Lord Jesus Christ is going to return, "God has not chosen to pour out his anger upon us, but to save us through our Lord Jesus Christ; he died for us so that we can live with him forever, whether we are dead or alive at the time of his return. So encourage each other to build each other up, just as you are already doing" (5:9-11).

GOD'S PURPOSE
"For God has not chosen to pour out his anger upon us, but to save us through our Lord Jesus Christ" (5:9). God did not "appoint us to wrath" (KJV). The word "appoint" or "choose" is the key word. In the original language, it meant "to place" or "to put." For instance, I place my Bible before me so I can read it. There is a purpose behind my putting it there. God did not place us in a position of wrath. God's plan does not call for us to experience the wrath that must come on those who reject

him. It is God's purpose that we receive not wrath, but salvation through Jesus Christ the Lord.

Salvation is not dependent upon man's initiative, but God's. God seeks man. God draws man to himself.

The word "wrath" (KJV) or "anger" simply means God's divine displeasure or judgment. Some say, "If God is a God of love, he cannot be a God of wrath." That is not true. Only one who loves deeply is capable of deep anger. Only one who knows true holiness is capable of understanding the awfulness of evil. A God of love and compassion must also have deep hatred for evil. Love does not ignore evil and condone rebellion. Because God loves deeply and completely, wrath will come to everyone who rejects him. Apart from him we will suffer hell. God loves us because he knows where we are headed without him. When we reject his love, we experience his wrath. But God did not choose us for that.

Someone says, "A good God would not send a man to hell." Absolutely not! God does not want anyone to go to hell. God does not want us to suffer anguish in our lives. He does not want us to be discouraged, depressed, defeated.

Rather, he wants us to receive salvation through Jesus Christ. That is the purpose of all God has done in history. "Salvation" (KJV) means to save from acute physical danger. It refers secularly to someone gaining release from imminent danger or from some threat. In the theological and biblical sense it means to be delivered from the wrath of God and the inevitable consequences of our sin, to be released, to be set free, to walk with peace in our hearts and a song on our lips. We walk with confidence into the uncertainty of the future, knowing that he is there.

How can God give us eternal life? By giving us Jesus Christ. Jesus said, "The time is coming, in fact, it is here, when the dead shall hear my voice—the voice of the Son of God—and those who listen shall live. The Father has life in himself, and has granted his Son to have life in himself" (John 5:25, 26). He has life in himself, and salvation is ours when he gives himself to us.

Salvation is not to be found in man's ingenuity, nor in man's adherence to certain rituals or organized worship. It is found only in Jesus Christ. He is the one who brings purpose and meaning to all that we do in worship and religion. We serve the same Jesus Christ the Thessalonians served. He is the same yesterday, today, and forever. That same Jesus who moved in mighty power in the first century still moves today. He is still the author and finisher of salvation. He is still the one who brings meaning and purpose to life. He is still the one who gives an unquenchable, unconquerable faith and hope to those who receive him. God does not want to give us his wrath, but his Son.

As Christians we will not receive the judgment of God upon an unbelieving world. There is no condemnation for those who have found life in Christ Jesus (Rom. 8:1).

CHRIST'S PURCHASE
Verse 10 is the only place in these two epistles where Paul specifically states that Christ died for us. It is woven

throughout these epistles, but here he plainly declares it so there could be no misunderstanding. By his death on the cross, Jesus Christ purchased our souls and our salvation. He paid the price for us.

"He died for us" could be translated, "He died concerning us" or "He died in the interest of us." In other words, he died on our behalf. His death has consequences for us. The death of Jesus Christ is not simply one experience in history, not simply a tragedy at the end of a beautiful life. His death has specific, eternal implications to us today. His death was in our best interests. This is the deep significance of the cross.

We do not have to suffer the anguish and agony of separation from God. We do not have to suffer the despair and frustration of life without God. Jesus has purchased our salvation.

"Who died for us, that, whether we wake or sleep, we should live together with him" (5:10, KJV). Whether we are alive or dead, we will live together with him. "Wake" is the same word that is translated "watch" in verse 6. Those believers who are alive are expecting Christ to come.

Paul is declaring that when we are saved, we have a relationship with Jesus Christ that death cannot affect. Death cannot do anything to our relationship with Christ. Whether we live or die, whether we are alive when we hear the trumpet sound or whether we are dead and our bodies awake to the resurrection call, it makes no difference. We have an eternal relationship with Jesus Christ, and death cannot disrupt it.

Some of us are not as healthy as we used to be. We are

all moving toward a date with physical death. But whether we live or die, we will live forever with Jesus Christ. Praise God! We have been redeemed for all eternity.

THE CHRISTIAN'S PRIORITY

Verse 9 speaks of God's purpose, verse 10 of Christ's purchase, verse 11 of our priority: "So encourage each other to build each other up, just as you are already doing." Our priority is to be our fellowship with and encouragement of each other. Whenever we are out of sorts, and things are not right in our fellowship, and there is anger in our hearts, we are on thin ice.

"Who died for us that, whether we wake or sleep, we should live together with him. Wherefore comfort yourselves together, and edify one another" (5:10, 11, KJV). Together, yourselves, one another. Over and over again we find emphasis on the priority of our mutual responsibility to each other, our love for each other, our concern for each other.

Some people say, "The church does not minister to me." But we are in this together. The preacher isn't a superior Christian who has achieved all the answers and has no hurts, no problems, no pain. We need each other. We need to encourage each other, love each other, guide each other, pray for each other. This is top priority.

He says, "We can live with him forever" (5:10). The King James Version uses the word "together." The entire verse speaks of a reunion. Every one of us can go to a cemetery plot somewhere and stand beside a grave and know that in that place the body of someone we love awaits the resurrection call. Hallelujah!

In 1 Corinthians 15, the Apostle Paul declared that no two heavenly bodies are the same. Each one is unique and distinct. "So also is the resurrection of the dead" (1 Cor. 15:42, KJV). When we rise to meet the Lord, we shall rise with distinctive and individual bodies and identities. We shall live together with him.

"Encourage" (5:11) means "to exhort, to strengthen." Literally, the word means "to strengthen someone by our words," by what we say. Would it not be marvelous if all the words we spoke to each other were strengthening and supportive words!

"Encourage" and "build up" are both present imperatives. They speak of a binding obligation that is continuous. This is to be the habitual pattern of our lives.

"The body is not one member, but many. If the foot shall say, Because I am not the hand, I am not of the body; is it therefore not of the body? . . . But now hath God set the members every one of them in the body, as it hath pleased him" (1 Cor. 12:14-18, KJV).

We encourage the members of our body to work together so that no members are pained or deprived. It should be so in the body of Christ. We are to encourage, lift up, strengthen each other.

"Build each other up." There is nothing static about the Christian faith. There must be continuous progress toward maturity. It has been my observation that people who talk about how mature they are really do not know how immature they are! Spiritual growth and maturity are lifelong experiences.

After thirty years of the most effective evangelistic work the world has ever seen, the Apostle Paul said, "No, dear brothers, I am still not all I should be but I am bringing all my energies to bear on this one thing: Forgetting the past and looking forward to what lies ahead, I strain to reach the end of the race and receive the prize for which God is calling us up to heaven because of what Christ Jesus did for us" (Phil. 3:13, 14). We either progress or regress. We move on or slide back. Let the man who thinks he stands take heed, lest he fall (1 Cor. 10:12).

"Now therefore, you are no more strangers and foreigners, but fellow citizens with the saints, and of the household of God; and are built upon the foundation of the apostles and prophets, Jesus Christ himself being the chief corner stone; in whom all the building fitly framed together groweth unto a holy temple in the Lord: in whom ye also are builded together for an habitation of God through the Spirit" (Eph. 2:19-22, KJV). "Ye also, as lively stones, are built up a spiritual house, a holy priesthood" (1 Pet. 2:5, KJV).

"Even as also ye do" (KJV) tells us the Thessalonians were already encouraging each other. But Paul is telling them to keep it up. We never reach a time when we can stop comforting and edifying each other.

17
Wholehearted Love
First Thessalonians 5:12-15

"Dear brothers, honor the officers of your church who work hard among you and warn you against all that is wrong. Think highly of them and give them your wholehearted love because they are straining to help you. And remember, no quarreling among yourselves. Dear brothers, warn those who are lazy; comfort those who are frightened; take tender care of those who are weak; and be patient with everyone. See that no one pays back evil for evil, but always try to do good to each other and to everyone else" (5:12-15).

THE PASSION
The first part of this passage concerns the leaders of the church—deacons, teachers, all who are in leadership responsibilities in the church. He is not just speaking about the pastor or one of the ministers, but of all who are serving and sharing through the leadership of the church.

Wholehearted Love

The phrase "think highly of them" is an adverbial phrase found only here in the New Testament, though one of the words is used elsewhere with a different Greek ending. It helps us understand how strong our love and encouragement ought to be for those who lead us. "Now glory be to God who by his mighty power at work within us is able to do far more than we would ever dare to ask or even dream of—infinitely beyond our *highest* ["exceeding abundantly above all" (KJV)] prayers, desires, thoughts, or hopes" (Eph. 3:20). Paul uses a strong word to motivate passionate support for church leaders.

"Dear brothers" reminds us that we share something in common. We have a common Savior. We have been forgiven of our sins. We are brothers and sisters in Christ. We share an eternal relationship.

This should make it easy to support our leaders, and each other. Much of the time, we do not honor those who lead us in the church. Paul urges us to fully appreciate their value and their worth.

Now he says, "Honor the officers... who work hard among you." "Work hard" comes from a word which means to toil to the point of weariness, to wear oneself out. Those who serve God in leadership capacity through the church often give themselves tirelessly and without concern for their own welfare. They labor to the point of exhaustion.

Do you aspire to be a leader in the church? Are you a leader in the church? Then God expects you to wear yourself out. There is no room for laziness in the kingdom. There is no room for people who will not fulfill their responsibilities. Energy alone does not make one a spiritual leader, but a true spiritual leader will be tirelessly energetic.

This does not mean that we have a group of spiritual bosses in the church. We all share a common responsibility, but there are some whom God has placed in a position of responsibility. We are to know them for what they are worth. We are to appreciate them for their value. They admonish us and challenge us. They direct us and encourage us in the decisions that we need to make. Thus, we are to "give them our wholehearted love because they are straining to help us." We are told to "think highly of them." We must get our heads straight about those who are leading us, whether it be a Sunday school teacher, a deacon, a pastor, or a minister.

How we think and feel about those who lead in the church is not to be based on their personal character or worth, or whether we like them or not. We are to think highly of them "for their work's sake" (KJV).

If we will do this, it will change our lives. We will view the work of God through the church in its proper perspective. The important thing is not the personal satisfaction or ego of any leader of the church, but the welfare of the church. It is the ministry we have together that should cause us to think highly and to love those whom God has given to us.

God does not use any of us because we deserve it. If God ever started disqualifying us because of a lack of personal worth, none of us would be left. No preacher would stand in the pulpit, no minister would serve on the staff, no deacon would minister through the church, no teacher would deliver a lesson.

As we encourage and love each other and do what God has entrusted us to do, it will be amazing how much liberty the Holy Spirit will have to change us and make us the kind of people we ought to be. None of us have arrived. God is still dealing with us all, Christian leaders included.

Paul continues, "And remember, no quarreling among yourselves." We cannot preach love effectively if there is an atmosphere of hostility and hatred. We cannot preach peace convincingly in an atmosphere of chaos and turmoil. So Paul reminds us to "be at peace among yourselves" (KJV).

THE PURSUIT
"We exhort you, brethren" (5:14, KJV). It is not enough for us to think rightly about the leadership of the church. It is not enough for us to give them honor and respect. We must share the ministry with them. The responsibility for the fellowship of the church is just as surely yours as it is the pastor's. We all have a responsibility to minister.

We are to "warn those who are lazy." "Lazy" is a military word which originally referred to someone who was out of step in a parade or march. It pictured disarray and a lack of discipline. From there it came to mean idleness or laziness. There were people in Thessalonica who had quit their jobs and were letting others support them while they waited for the Lord to come. God expects us to work physically, and spiritually too. God never intended for any of his children not to be growing and aggressive in their faith.

"Comfort those who are frightened." We are to comfort the fainthearted, encourage those who are discouraged.

"Take tender care of those who are weak." Our job is to encourage each other, not to push someone down because they are less than what they ought to be. We are to lift them up, encourage them, and help them to grow. When a brother stumbles, we are to pick him up and restore him. Furthermore, we are to "be patient with everyone."

We are not to be unkind toward each other. We are to be patient. We are not to seek to satisfy our ego or to vindicate our character. We are to love and let God lead.

THE PRINCIPLE

Now Paul gives a principle of living. "See that no one pays back evil for evil, but always try to do good to each other and to everyone else" (5:15). The church in Thessalonica was being persecuted by both Gentiles and Jews. It was hard for them not to react. People were criticizing and condemning them. People were threatening their lives and confiscating their property. Paul says to not return evil for evil.

Jesus in the Gospels, and the Apostle Paul and the other writers of the New Testament have set forth this same principle: There is *never* an occasion for retaliation! God will vindicate us. God will do his work. If someone

Wholehearted Love

is unkind to us, we must not be unkind to them. If someone hates us, do not hate them back. If someone strikes us, we must not strike them back. If someone steals from us, we are not to steal in return. Do not repay evil for evil.

If the church today could build itself upon this principle, it would revolutionize our communities. Do not repay evil for evil, but "always try to do good." We are to repay evil with good. There are lots of times we could fight back, but vengeance belongs to God and he will repay. If we are his and everything we have belongs to him, then every difficulty also belongs to him. He will take care of it.

We are to do this not only with Christians but with non-Christians too, not just in the fellowship of the church, but out in the city.

The reason we can repay evil with good is because that is what Jesus did for us. We were sinners, and as sinners we opposed everything Jesus stood for. Every ounce of energy that drove those nails into his hands, every muscle that forced those thorns into his brow, every bit of energy that caused the spear to be pushed into his side, all of the cursing and spitting, the plucking of the beard from his face—all of it was because of our sins. We did it! We killed him! And he loved us in spite of it. He repayed evil with love. Now he says, "You do the same thing."

Urgent
Admonitions
*First
Thessalonians
5:16-22*

"Always be joyful" reminds us of the disposition that God has planted in the heart of the Christian. It is significant that God placed that verse immediately after a warning about retaliation and our response to mistreatment. In essence Paul says, "Do not return evil for evil, but return good to them and rejoice in the midst of it."

HAPPY PRAYER
First of all, we are to "Always be joyful. Always keep on praying. No matter what happens, always be thankful." A genuine church of God is first of all a happy church. God forbid that we should look as if somebody just died when we come together in the church. We are to be a rejoicing church. There are some stern realities in life and some sobering admonitions that God gives to us, but the Christian life is most of all a happy life.

A genuine church is also a praying church and, thirdly, a thankful church. The church is always to major in gratitude to God. We are not to grumble and complain, or fight, criticize, and condemn, but always and in all things to express gratitude to God for what he is doing.

"*Always* be joyful" (5:16). Everything in the Christian experience should be a cause for joy. Even though we are maligned, even though we are misunderstood, we can rejoice because we know God is still in control. We can rejoice in what God is doing in our lives and in what he is going to do.

This matter of rejoicing leaps at us throughout the New Testament. "Finally, my brethren, rejoice in the Lord" (Phil. 3:1, KJV). "Always be full of joy in the Lord; I say it again, rejoice!" (Phil. 4:4). When Paul speaks to ordained men about how they can prove their calling and demonstrate the presence of God in their lives, he says, "Our hearts ache, but at the same time we have the joy of the Lord" (2 Cor. 6:10).

This is in the imperative; thus if we refuse to do it, we are sinning. Sadsack Christianity is direct rebellion against the expressed will of God for our lives.

We somehow have the idea that the things we do wrong are worse than the good things we do not do. But some of the strongest language in the Bible is reserved for those who refuse to do what they ought to do. When the tribes of Reuben and Gad were about to let the other ten tribes go into the Promised Land and possess it without them, Joshua said to them, "But if you don't do as you have said, then you will have sinned against the Lord, and you may be sure that your sin will catch up with you" (Num. 32:23). This was a sin of omission, failing to do what they had been expressly commanded to do.

Rejoicing, praying, and being thankful to God are not options. They are not electives for the Christian life, things we can take or leave. We are talking about things that God has specifically commanded of us. If we do not do them, we sin.

"Always keep on praying" (5:17). "Praying" is the most comprehensive word for prayer in the Greek language. It referred to all kinds of prayer. In fact, in ancient times it referred to any prayers to any god. For the Christian, it spoke of personal communication with our God.

We are told to "pray without ceasing" (KJV). "Don't be weary in prayer; keep at it; watch for God's answers and remember to be thankful when they come" (Col. 4:2). "Pray all the time" (Eph. 6:18).

We can pray anywhere, anytime. We do not have to be on our knees to pray. The doors of heaven are never closed; God's ear is always open. There may be times when we don't verbalize our prayer, but the spirit and attitude of prayer is to be continually a part of our experience. Literally this means, "Do not abandon praying. Never stop praying." Yet we would sooner miss an appointment with a doctor than to miss an appointment with God.

Individually we are to be praying, but also the church collectively is to continually be praying. An intercessory prayer ministry is one of the most important things a church can do.

There is not one of us who cannot pray. Perhaps we cannot teach or sing, but we can pray. Some of us may not physically be able to walk down a street to visit others, but we can pray. None is incapable of prayer.

*Urgent
Admonitions*

The greatest sadness any church could have would not be to lose half of its membership, or to fail in some of its church programs, but to fail to pray.

"No matter what happens, always be thankful." Every experience, every circumstance is an occasion for praising and thanking God. You may think, "But you don't know my problems!" You don't know mine either! But we are not the only ones with problems. We are not the only ones who ever face disappointments or sadness. We are not the only ones who ever lost a job or a friendship. We are not the only ones who have been lied about. God says, "No matter what happens, always be thankful."

Do you know why God can say that? He knows how it is going to come out! He knows what is going to happen next! All we know is our disappointment or discouragement or despair, but God knows that is not the end of the story. He is working things out for our best interest.

"And we know that all that happens to us is working for our good if we love God and are fitting into his plans. ... Who then can ever keep Christ's love from us? When we have trouble or calamity, when we are hunted down or destroyed, is it because he doesn't love us anymore? And if we are hungry, or penniless, or in danger, or threatened with death, has God deserted us?... But despite all this, overwhelming victory is ours through Christ who loved us enough to die for us. For I am convinced that nothing can ever separate us from his love. Death can't, and life can't. The angels won't, and all the powers of hell itself cannot keep God's love away. Our fears for today, our worries about tomorrow, or where we are—high above the sky, or in the deepest ocean—

nothing will ever be able to separate us from the love of God demonstrated by our Lord Jesus Christ when he died for us" (Romans 8:28, 35, 37-39). In all of these terrible things that we so often struggle through, we can have overwhelming victory.

Nothing can separate us from God's love. Nothing can detour his purposes in us. He may allow some things to come that are hard for us to face, but as we face them with rejoicing, as we face them praying, as we face them thanking God, he is able to turn them around and achieve his best purposes through us.

Do not despair when the cross gets heavy, do not despair when the burden is oppressive, for it may be at that moment that God is perfecting the greatest blessing of heaven to place into your life.

HEEDED PROCLAMATION

"Do not smother the Holy Spirit. Do not scoff at those who prophesy" (5:19, 20). You have heard many sermons preached on smothering or "quenching" the Holy Spirit. But this statement is tied to this specific Scripture, "Do not scoff at those who prophesy." Do not quench the Spirit by belittling prophecy—that is the point.

The historical setting is helpful here. The Thessalonian believers were new converts who did not have the advantage of a completed Bible. During the years when God was compiling, by the inspiration of the Holy Spirit, what we call the New Testament, there were prophets who were given to the early church so that God could

*Urgent
Admonitions*

speak through those prophets directly to the people. They had no New Testament as we do. So God sent prophets with a direct word from him.

The word "prophet" involves "forthtelling." He tells forth the word of God. It is not to be equated with ESP or predicting the future, though there was some foretelling or predictive element in prophesying on occasion. Most of the time, prophecy involved declaring the whole counsel of God, including the great themes of redemption and the purposes of God.

In Thessalonica some of the believers had evidently heard so many false prophets, they began to discount all prophets. So Paul called for a balance on this. He is saying, "Don't belittle a word that comes from God, because you are belittling the Holy Spirit."

We are not to turn away from the counsel of God's Word that comes to us and from the moving of the Spirit of God in us. We can quench the Spirit by ignoring God's Word.

Prophecy that is given today is the expounding of the Word of God. When the Holy Spirit begins to apply biblical truth to our lives, we must not quench the Spirit by turning away.

HEALTHY POSITION

"Test everything that is said to be sure it is true" (5:21). There were false prophets preaching in Thessalonica. Paul commanded the believers to test these prophets. Was there ever a time when there was more heresy proclaimed in the name of God and the Bible than today? How do we test the prophecy? Remember, God will never tell us something new that contradicts what he has already spoken. Paul was saying, "Take every prophecy that is given and if it contradicts the Old Testament Scriptures or the word of the apostles that you have received, then reject it." For us, this means that if we hear something that contradicts the Word of God, we are to reject it. If it does not parallel the Word of God, do not have anything to do with it.

"Hold fast that which is good" (KJV). "Hold fast" is a strong word. It means to latch onto, glue yourself to, not turn loose. There is enough evil floating around. Leave it alone and hold on to right, that which is healthy and whole. When something is proven to be true, then "accept it."

We are further to "keep away from every kind of evil" (5:22). That word "keep away from" is the same word that Paul used earlier when he said, "Keep clear of all sexual sin" (4:3). It is a strong word. This word has a preposition prefixed to it, making it even stronger. It means to separate ourselves from all appearance of evil, from every kind of evil, from every expression of evil.

19
Complete Devotion to God
First Thessalonians 5:23-28

In this final passage of 1 Thessalonians, one of the most important of the entire book, the Apostle Paul wraps up all that he has been talking about.

"May the God of peace himself make you entirely pure and devoted to God; and may your spirit and soul and body be kept strong and blameless until that day when our Lord Jesus Christ comes back again. God, who called you to become his child, will do all this for you, just as he promised. Dear brothers, pray for us. Shake hands for me with all the brothers there. I command you in the name of the Lord to read this letter to all the Christians. And may rich blessings from our Lord Jesus Christ be with you, every one" (5:23-28).

Verse 23, the key to the passage, indicates that the totality of our being is involved in our being saved. Our relationship with God involves our minds, bodies, hearts, and everything we are or ever shall be. It has to do with every area of our lives.

*Complete
Devotion to God*

THE CALL TO EXCEL

"May the God of peace himself make you entirely pure and devoted to God; and may your spirit and soul and body be kept strong and blameless until that day when our Lord Jesus Christ comes back again" (5:23). God calls us to excel in spiritual living. In the Sermon on the Mount, Jesus called upon the disciples to have a righteousness exceeding that of hypocritical leaders, the subjects of our Lord's strongest attacks. "But I warn you —unless your goodness is greater than that of the Pharisees and other Jewish leaders, you can't get into the Kingdom of Heaven" (Matt. 5:20).

He went on to command that we love our enemies and bless those who have cursed us, because "If you love only those who love you, what good is that? Even scoundrels do that much. If you are friendly only to your friends, how are you different from anyone else? Even the heathen do that. But you are to be perfect, even as your Father in heaven is perfect" (Matt. 5:46-48). The word "perfect" means to be complete, to realize the purpose for which we were created. The call of Jesus Christ is a call to excel, to be different, to rise above the garbage of the earth, to rise above the polluted attitudes of those around us.

The prophet Isaiah said that we were to mount up with wings like eagles (40:31). Why did he not say, "Wings of buzzards or sparrows"? Why eagles? The eagle is destined to soar in the heavens. There is to be no polluted atmosphere for the eagle. His home is in the pure air of the heights. The call of God to us is to excel, to rise above.

Notice where this call comes from: "the very God of

peace" (KJV) or literally, "the God of peace himself." All through 1 Thessalonians the Apostle Paul has challenged the Christians to live a certain way, but the only hope they have of doing it is for God himself to live it through them.

"Peace" means complete prosperity, complete satisfaction of the whole person, fulfillment. If we are going to know that kind of peace, God is going to have to produce it in us.

This call to excel is a call for us to yield our lives to God, so he can do in us what we cannot do in our own strength. Only God can bring spiritual satisfaction and wholeness to our lives.

"The very God of peace himself sanctify you wholly" (5:23, KJV). "Sanctify" means "to be set apart for God." Our total person, through and through, is set apart for God. That includes the way we think, the way we act, the way we dress, the way we work, the way we relate to each other. Is everything in our lives dedicated to the purposes of God? Our attitudes at home? Our attitudes at work? Our relationship with our friends and loved ones? God calls us to be set apart totally for him. The good news in this is that God will do the sanctifying. God will do in us what he calls us to do.

"And may your spirit and soul and body be kept strong and blameless until that day when our Lord Jesus Christ comes back again." Some people have seen in this verse a description of the trichotomy of the human personality: body, soul, and spirit. This could be, but what he is really saying is, "I am praying that God will take everything that you are, every facet of your life, and set it apart for his purposes." In other words, being saved means that the whole person is to go God's way unanimously. Our bodies, spirits, and souls are walking together. The unity idea is confirmed in that this compound subject has a singular verb.

"Preserved blameless" (KJV) tells us that God does not just want us to live a good life, but an exceptional one. Paul is not speaking of sinless perfection, but of fulfilling the purpose God has given to us. We are to be faithful servants until Christ comes.

What God does in our lives is not something he does for a while and then drops. He continues working in us right up to the coming of the Lord and into eternity. God holds us securely in his love and grace. It is good to know that our salvation is not dependent on our holding onto God, but on his holding onto us.

THE POWER TO EXCEL

How can I be what I know I ought to be? How can I do what I know I ought to do? How can I have the mind and the attitude and the spirit that I ought to have?

"God, who called you to become his child, will do all this for you, just as he promised" (5:24). God is always faithful to his word. What he started, he is going to finish. What he sets out to do, he will accomplish.

Paul declares that God cannot deny himself (2 Tim. 2:13, KJV). Even if we are unfaithful, God is faithful. God will keep his word. The power to live the life that excels is found in the faithfulness of God. We are saved not because we feel pious, or because we decide we are going to change the way we live. We are saved because God himself plants his Spirit within us, and our assurance is based on what God has said.

God not only is a caller, but a doer; not only a talker, but a performer. "God will do all this for you" (5:24). What God calls us to do, he will perform through us.

Do we want a better life than we have? Do we want victory in areas where we have been defeated? Do we want comfort in areas where sorrow has torn our hearts apart? Do we want peace and ease instead of being depressed and discouraged? God can do all this. We cannot do it ourselves, but he is faithful to do it in us.

Sometimes we get wrapped up in discouragement and before we know it, we are bound by it and obsessed with it. How can we break free from thinking about things that depress us, discourage us, remind us of our weaknesses and our inadequacies?

Someone has suggested that our minds are like television screens, and there is always something on the screen. Even when we are asleep, it is subconsciously active. If we had to watch television and could not turn it off, what would be our only other option? Obviously, it would be to change channels.

That is what God does in our lives. "Thy word have I hid in mine heart, that I might not sin against thee" (Psalm 119:11, KJV). As we memorize, study, and meditate on the Word of God, God programs our minds. When depression and discouragement come, we can greet them with a verse of Scripture and with a song of victory in our hearts. God brings us triumph because "faithful is he that calleth you, who also will do it" (5:24, KJV).

Some of us have just enough religion to make us miserable. We have made just enough commitment to keep us unhappy. We are not really willing to be all that God wants us to be. We want to be average, but the call of God is to excel. We should excel in love, patience, understanding, compassion, evangelistic fervor. And praise God, what he calls us to do, he gives us the power to do.

THE FELLOWSHIP TO EXCEL

We cannot excel by ourselves. We need each other. "Dear brothers, pray for us. Shake hands for me with all the brothers there. I command you in the name of the Lord to read this letter to all the Christians. And may rich blessings from our Lord Jesus Christ be with you, every one" (5:25-28).

"Pray for us." Sometimes we think of the Apostle Paul as a missionary superhero, an evangelistic superman. He went around telling everybody what to do, organizing churches, knocking down strongholds of Satan. What a man! Always on the go. Always on top of everything. In truth, the Apostle Paul was a man like you and me. He was a man who was often discouraged. Sometimes he had misgivings about the wisdom of the decisions that he had made. He was a man with the same kind of struggles that we have. This great apostle who penned for us at least thirteen of the books of the New Testament asked new converts to "pray for us."

None of us can make it by ourselves. We all need the power of God in our lives. Each one of us needs the intercession and fellowship of each other as well.

God wants us to love each other, encourage each other, and pray for each other. Christian fellowship is not optional. There is no such thing as a victorious freelance Christian. God has given us the church. We require its fellowship.

"Greet all the brethren with a holy kiss" (5:25, KJV). The kiss on the cheek was a greeting, somewhat like shaking hands today or saying hello. In the East it was a salutatory formality.

Paul is saying, "Your greeting should be not just a mere form. Greet others not just with a kiss, but a holy kiss. I want you to really love them, to really be interested in them."

In the fellowship of the church there ought to be such a deep and genuine interest in each other that even our greetings are warm and compassionate. There ought to be a fellowship deeper than that of the world. Sometimes we get careless about greeting people too casually. God reminds us to let the greeting be genuine.

"I command you" (5:27) is a very strong word. He commands them to read this epistle to the church. "To read" is a Greek word that means to read aloud. Why aloud? He has dealt with some very important truths here. He wanted to be sure the believers heard them personally.

Also, accusers of the Apostle Paul had told these new Christians that Paul didn't really love them. By having this read aloud, Paul would be assured that the critics would be silenced as the Spirit of God used the words that he wrote.

"The grace of our Lord Jesus Christ be with you" (5:28, KJV). God's grace is what saves and keeps us. Our entire spiritual life—and our fellowship together—is due to the grace of God.

From start to finish, the call of God to our lives is a call to rise above the habits of the world. It is a call to give ourselves—body, spirit, and soul—to the purposes of God.

2 THESSALONIANS

A Growing Faith
Second Thessalonians 1:1-4

In 2 Thessalonians, Paul deals with some of the same subjects as in the first letter, but in greater detail. He starts off by complimenting the Thessalonian church, a church loaded with problems. The Apostle Paul was a man who looked for the good in the midst of the bad.

We are just the opposite. If we can find something to gripe about, we will. If there is anything to be unhappy about, we will zero in on it. But we do not find in these early verses any hint of condemnation.

"From: Paul, Silas and Timothy. To: The church of Thessalonica—kept safe in God our Father and in the Lord Jesus Christ. May God the Father and the Lord Jesus Christ give you rich blessings and peace-filled hearts and minds. Dear brothers, giving thanks to God for you is not only the right thing to do, but it is our duty to God, because of the really wonderful way your faith has grown, and because of your growing love for each other. We are happy to tell other churches about your

A Growing Faith

patience and complete faith in God, in spite of all the crushing troubles and hardships you are going through" (1:1-4).

THE REASON
The Thessalonians' faith had no reason to grow, from a human standpoint at least. They lived in a pagan society, in the midst of Greek philosophers with agnostic and atheistic attitudes. There was strong opposition to the idea of one God and to the idea of his Son, Jesus Christ, coming into the world.

How could their faith grow in an atmosphere like that? What encouragement could they possibly have?

Paul calls God "our Father." In 1 Thessalonians 1:1 he said, "God *the* Father." Paul is identifying both the recipients of the letter and his missionary group as being children of the same Father, and thus part of the same faith.

He says, "May God give you rich blessings and peace-filled hearts and minds." The King James Version says, "grace and peace." Grace is unearned favor or kindness. Peace is inner tranquillity and inner wholeness of life.

Paul identifies the basis of this grace and peace. It comes from God and our Lord Jesus Christ. In fact, it can be found nowhere else. Men can find peace of heart, soul, and mind only in God.

We are living today in the most affluent, most enlightened age ever. We have achieved more with natural science, human logic, and intellect than ever before. Yet today we have the highest crime rate, the highest suicide rate, the highest divorce rate, the highest drug rate in the history of the world. Why? Because our men and women reject Jesus Christ, Prince of Peace.

How does faith grow? God makes it grow.

THE REQUIREMENT
"Dear brothers, giving thanks to God for you is not only the right thing to do, but it is our duty to God, because of the really wonderful way your faith has grown, and because of your growing love for each other" (1:3). Giving thanks is our "duty." That is a strong word. Paul says, "We have an obligation to thank God for you."

Such thanksgiving was "the right thing to do." They would be amiss if they did not do it. The idea here is of continual thanks. They were to always thank God for the believers.

Would it not be marvelous if we would constantly and continually pray for each other! We should pray for people who differ with us, people who may have personalities that grate on us, people we do not like. We need to pray for each other.

We cannot be angry and bitter toward someone we pray for. The best medicine for resentment, bitterness, hostility, and anger against others is to pray for them. This is why Jesus said we ought to pray for our enemies. If we don't pray for them, how can we love them?

A Growing Faith

The phrase "the really wonderful way your faith has grown" means that it has grown beyond measure. It was growing, blossoming, maturing faith.

Their love toward each other was also growing, and overflowing. The greatest thing we can offer to people around us is to care about them, to love them.

It is interesting that what he is saying here is the answer to his earlier prayer: "And may the Lord make your love to grow and overflow to each other and to everyone else, just as our love does toward you" (1 Thess. 3:12). That was his prayer several months before. Now he writes to say that God has heard and answered. Their love was a direct answer to his prayer.

THE RESULTS
"We are happy to tell other churches about your patience and complete faith in God, in spite of all the crushing troubles and hardships you are going through" (1:4). Paul was bragging about the Thessalonians to other churches, telling everyone about them.

Apparently in the two or three months that had transpired since 1 Thessalonians had been written, word had come to the Apostle Paul that the Christians in Thessalonica were discouraged. They had misgivings about their effectiveness in that community. They began to wonder about their spiritual lives.

The Apostle Paul was saying in effect, "I know that you have a love and faith that is growing. We are proud of you. We are even bragging about you to the other churches." Those other churches were probably in the region around Corinth, the area where Paul was serving at that time.

Paul was bragging about their "patience." "Patience" does not simply mean to endure something, to passively wait for it to be over. "Patience" means to take hold of a problem and master it, to face a problem victoriously, to take our difficulties, disappointments, and discouragements and, rather than simply living through them, come out victorious over them. We can have a patience that conquers, a life that is undefeated. We are not simply waiting for something to be over; we are "more than conquerors" (Rom. 8:37, KJV).

The Thessalonian Christians were patient in the midst of all the pressures that were thrust upon them. They were master of their circumstances. Their patience and faith brought glorious victory.

"We are happy to tell other churches about your patience and complete faith in God, in spite of all the crushing troubles and hardships." "All" implies many problems, but they were able to cope in Christ.

"Going through" is in the present tense in the Greek language. They had had many problems, and they were not over yet.

No one ever gets away from problems or disappointments. If we have not had a heartache recently, hang on—we will. Even getting saved doesn't end our problems. In fact, when we come to Christ, we not only get a new friend, but a new enemy. Satan makes sure we have problems and difficulties.

But the Christian does have someone to work through

his problems for him. They are no longer our problems but his. We belong to him. God will carry us through. He will face our problems with us and for us.

Sometimes the road gets rough. But God is still the same. He can still bring victory through any circumstances. We must first commit our lives to Christ, then obey him if he is to bring us victory in the midst of every pressure, every persecution, every tribulation that we face.

21
The Righteous Judgment of God
Second Thessalonians 1:5-10

"This is only one example of the fair, just way God does things, for he is using your sufferings to make you ready for his kingdom, while at the same time he is preparing judgment and punishment for those who are hurting you. And so I would say to you who are suffering, God will give you rest along with us when the Lord Jesus appears suddenly from heaven in flaming fire with his mighty angels, bringing judgment on those who do not wish to know God, and who refuse to accept his plan to save them through our Lord Jesus Christ. They will be punished in everlasting hell, forever separated from the Lord, never to see the glory of his power, when he comes to receive praise and admiration because of all he has done for his people, his saints. And you will be among those praising him, because you have believed what we told you about him" (1:5-10).

This passage brings a tremendous encouragement to our hearts, for suffering is something that afflicts us all. Disappointments, depression, despair, and discouragement come to all of us. Then, too, some endeavor to destroy our faith. Paul's words to the Thessalonians can be a great help to us as well.

Verse 5 immediately confronts us with the difference in the way we look at suffering and the way God looks at it. Any time we encounter disappointment or persecution or trouble, we automatically assume it is bad and we will go to any lengths to get away from it.

But God's Word tells us that trouble is not always what it seems to be. It is not always the triumph of evil. It is not always Satan getting his way. The apostle declares that suffering is God's way of preparing us for God's kingdom. The words "only one example" reveal that here is positive proof that God is "fair" and "just." The King James Version translates this, "a manifest token of the righteous judgment of God." When God gives us strength in the midst of our trials and troubles, when he gives us victory in our discouragements and despair, it is proof that God is working in our lives. God allows pressures to come into our lives so he can work in our hearts.

THE REASONS FOR HIS JUDGMENTS

The words "righteous judgment" (KJV) or "fair, just way" simply mean that God is always going to do the right thing. We never have to worry about God being unjust or unfair. Such judgment means two things: the vindication of godliness and retribution for evil.

Notice that this judgment makes us "ready for God's

kingdom." When we suffer, God's righteous judgment will not forget us. Sometimes we think nobody else knows the things which are crushing our souls. We may think we are alone in our pain, but God sees and understands. God's righteous judgment sees our sufferings. Rather than being a means of punishment, our suffering will usher us into the kingdom. It is God's way of preparing us for the kingdom.

The Christian faith is not too fragile to stand a few bumps, too sensitive to withstand disappointments. Genuine faith in Christ can stand up under the bombardments of doubt and temptation.

We have no choice as to whether or not we will have problems, difficulties, and troubles. They are inevitable. The faith that God has planted in us is in opposition to the world. We are to live for Christ in a hostile environment, so of course there will be problems. But rather than these problems defeating us, God can use them to equip us for spiritual victory now and life with him forever.

Verse 5 talks about God's judgment vindicating those who suffer. Verse 6 speaks of the righteous judgment of God bringing retribution to those who cause the suffering—"He is preparing judgment and punishment for those who are hurting you." God will judge anyone who causes us trouble, anyone Satan is using to harass and hound us. It is unnecessary for us to be angry and vindictive. We do not have to spend our lives seeking revenge. God says, "Vengeance is mine; I will repay" (Rom. 12:19, KJV). Because God's judgment is righteous, he vindicates the innocent and punishes the guilty.

*The Righteous
Judgment of God*

THE REVELATION OF HIS JUDGMENT

"And so I would say to you who are suffering, God will give you rest along with us when the Lord Jesus appears suddenly from heaven in flaming fire with his mighty angels" (1:7). The King James Version says, "revealed from heaven." "Revealed" is a frequent New Testament term meaning to unveil or uncover something that had been hidden. Today it seems to many that God is hidden to the world. It is not uncommon to hear someone say, "I do not believe in God. I see no evidence for his existence." But the Apostle Paul declares that an unveiling will come when the Lord Jesus will appear suddenly from heaven. The entire world will then see Jesus Christ for who he really is. The revelation of the righteous judgment of God will come for all to see.

"I would say to you who are suffering, God will give you rest along with us when the Lord Jesus appears." We can rest now because we know that when he comes again, things will be set straight. It is his work, not ours. It is God's gospel, not ours.

We spend most of our time worrying about things that are not really our problems. When we are in trouble, we focus on our problems. We get distressed. We get ulcers. We get nervous. We do all the things that everybody else does. God tells us not to worry because what happens to us is not our concern, but God's. God is saying, "Because you know I am a God of just and fair judgment, you can rest."

The idea of rest is the idea of being free from worry and bondage, free from that which would bind us and tie us down, free from concern that would destroy our happiness. Because God is a promise-keeping God, a God who will do what he has promised to do, we can rest easy and not spend our lives in anxiety.

Jesus put it, "So don't worry at all about having enough food and clothing. Why be like the heathen? For they take pride in all these things and are deeply concerned about them. But your heavenly Father already knows perfectly well that you need them, and he will give them to you if you give him first place in your life and live as he wants you to" (Matt. 6:31-33). We must let God develop peace in us so we can trust him.

"Flaming fire... bringing judgment" means that God's holiness is going to be vindicated. Now it seems as though a person can blaspheme God and get away with it, as though he can push God out of his life and nothing happens. But God will someday come in judgment.

We never get away with sin. We may think that what is done in secret remains secret, but God knows all. This passage is telling us that sin and judgment are inseparable. "Don't be misled; remember that you can't ignore God and get away with it: a man will always reap just the kind of crop he sows!" (Gal. 6:7).

Who will God take vengeance on? "Those who do not wish to know God, and who refuse to accept his plan to save them through our Lord Jesus Christ." If one does not know Jesus Christ, he is without excuse (Rom. 1:20). When Jesus Christ comes again, there will be righteous judgment upon those who have rejected him.

THE RESULTS OF HIS JUDGMENT

There are two results of the righteous judgment of God. First, "they will be punished in everlasting hell, forever separated from the Lord" (1:9, KJV).

Imagine the most horrible death possible. Now imagine it never ending. The punishment that God brings upon them is never-ending destruction. That means they will always be in the process of dying but never annihilated. They will spend eternity dying! What a tragedy for man to rebel against God! God declares that if we reject him, his righteous judgment will bring "everlasting destruction" (KJV).

Churches are lighthouses calling men to God. It is a fearful thing to fall into the hands of the living God. Our God is a consuming fire. The righteous judgment of God requires punishment of sin.

The destiny of unbelievers is eternal separation from God. Hell means that there is no God to comfort, no God to bless, no God to encourage! This is separation from "the glory of his power." I do not know how people can look at our world and assume that there is no God. Only the power of God keeps the stars in their orbit and keeps the laws of this world operating so that we can live and move. We cannot imagine the chaos, confusion, and despair that would inevitably accompany separation from the presence of God.

Some think that fire and destruction are just symbols, pictures of truth. But would we be afraid of a picture of fire? Of course not! Reality is worse than the picture. Whatever God is saying, if it is not literal fire it is worse than anything we could ever imagine. We would be fools not to fear the reality God is talking about here.

The second result of God's judgment will be that he will be praised "because of all he has done for his people, his saints" (1:10). When Jesus comes, he will "be glorified in his saints, and admired in all them that believe" (KJV). When Jesus returns, he will receive glory through us. We are his inheritance (Eph. 1:18). When we are saved, we get him and he gets us. When he comes back, every sinful impulse, every sinful natural instinct will be removed from us and we will be made like him for all eternity. We will bear his life perfectly, and he will be glorified in us. Thus, glory will be brought to him in us. The lost will be separated from God, but the saved will be a special glory and honor to God.

In the phrase "to be glorified in his saints," "saints" means those who are set apart for God's purposes. When we are saved, God purchases us and sets us apart for him. It is wrong for us to use our lives, bodies, and minds in ways contrary to the divine will.

But it also says, "to be admired in all them that *believe*." God sets us apart, but we are to embrace him in faith. Here is our part in the transaction. We are to deliberately trust him. God gives us salvation, but it is up to us to receive it. We must respond.

If there is in our hearts a desire to be saved, God put it there. If in our hearts there is a concern for our spiritual welfare, God put it there. We would have no concern at all if God did not give it to us.

The only way to be sure that when Christ comes he is going to be glorified in us is to do today what he wants us to do. We have no assurance that we will have another day. Now is the time of salvation. "And since Christ is so much superior, the Holy Spirit warns us to listen to him, to be careful to hear his voice today and not let our hearts become set against him, as the people of Israel did. They steeled themselves against his love and complained against him in the desert while he was testing them" (Heb. 3:7, 8).

The choice is ours. What will we do with Christ? Remember, he is a righteous judge. Because he is righteous, he cannot overlook our sins. And because he is righteous, he cannot fail to vindicate our faithfulness.

22
Glorifying the Name of Jesus
Second Thessalonians 1:11, 12

"And so we keep on praying for you that our God will make you the kind of children he wants to have—will make you as good as you wish you could be!—rewarding your faith with his power. Then everyone will be praising the name of the Lord Jesus Christ because of the results they see in you; and your greatest glory will be that you belong to him. The tender mercy of our God and of the Lord Jesus Christ has made all this possible for you" (1:11, 12).

These verses are bathed in prayer. Paul prays that the Thessalonians may so live for God that God will say, "You are my kind of people," that God will do his works in their lives.

"We keep on praying for you." This was continual, perpetual, daily prayer. We need to always pray for each other. We must constantly be in contact with God in prayer, interceding for others, praising God, thanking God, beseeching God.

The greatest thing we can do for each other is pray. The greatest thing you can do for your pastor is to pray for him. The greatest thing you can do for your nation is to pray for its leaders and its people. When we stop praying, we are saying that we do not need God, that he is unnecessary and that we can handle things without him. For many people prayer is just an emergency move. Even an atheist will cry out to God in desperation. But God's people should walk and live in prayer. It ought to be a daily experience in our lives.

Prayer is personal—"for you"—and specific. Specific prayer is the only kind of prayer that honors God.

Many people are never aware that God has answered their prayer. If we pray, "Lord, bless the missionaries," how do we know when he does? "Lord, bless our church." How do we gauge that? "Lord, be with our pastor." How do we know whether he is or not? We pray so vaguely and so generally that it is an absolute impossibility for God to confirm an answer to our prayers. It is specific prayer that honors God. It is personal praying that lays hold of the power of heaven.

PERFORMANCE

God expects us to put feet to our prayers. God expects us to live what we are praying. If we say we love God, we should live like it. We may say, "I am concerned for people who have needs." God says, "Show it by the way you live."

"We keep on praying for you that our God will make you the kind of children he wants to have" (1:11). Paul is praying that God would look at their lives and know they were his children by the way they lived. Every person who has been saved ought to live like it.

The idea here is that every Christian, down deep inside, wants to honor God. But we all know that wanting to do something is not doing it. Many people want something, but are not willing to commit themselves to the discipline to bring it to pass. There are many carnal Christians who do not like the way they are. They are miserable in their faith. They know they are not living as God wants them to live. But knowing that and just wanting to do better does not change anything.

Paul prays that God "will make you as good as you wish you could be." In other words, "I am praying that God would fulfill in you that desire to be better, stronger, more mature."

Paul adds, "rewarding your faith with his power." If we are going to fulfill that high resolve in our hearts, God is going to have to do it. In our own strength, we cannot be what we ought to be. Only God can fulfill our desire and our faith with his power. Human ability and human power is incapable of bringing happiness, fulfillment, and satisfaction.

Is God working through you? Is God revealing his purposes through you?

It will not just happen. We cannot simply desire it. Everybody wants to be nicer, cleaner, smarter, but just wanting it does not make it happen. There has to be a commitment that will allow God to work.

We are totally dependent upon God. We cannot live a Christian life, do the right things, react the right way, have the spirit we should have without God's help.

Paul speaks of "rewarding your faith with power." Faith is not lazy or idle. Faith *works*. We sometimes talk about faith as though it were something we could possess, like a pair of shoes or a set of keys in our pocket. It is not like that at all. It is not an addendum to our lives.

"Dear brothers, what's the use of saying that you have faith and are Christians if you aren't proving it by helping others? Will that kind of faith save anyone?" (James 2:14). A faith that is available for God to move through us is a working faith, a faith that produces good works.

"So you see, it isn't enough to just have faith. You must also do good to prove that you have it. Faith that doesn't show itself by good works is no faith at all—it is dead and useless. But someone may well argue, 'You say the way to God is by faith alone, plus nothing; well, I say that good works are important too, for without good works you can't prove whether you have faith or not; but anyone can see that I have faith by the way I act' " (James 2:17, 18).

The Apostle Paul also wrote, "Because of his kindness you have been saved through trusting Christ. And even trusting is not of yourselves; it too is a gift from God. Salvation is not a reward for the good we have done, so none of us can take any credit for it" (Eph. 2:8, 9). We stop there, but the thought continues: "It is God himself who has made us what we are and given us new lives from Christ Jesus; and long ages ago he planned that we should spend these lives in helping others" (Eph. 2:10).

Faith that saves is busy serving God. Anybody who

tells us he has faith in God and yet does not want to serve him is lying to us and to himself. It cannot be.

PRAISE
"Then everyone will be praising the name of the Lord Jesus Christ because of the results they see in you; and your greatest glory will be that you belong to him. The tender mercy of our God and of the Lord Jesus Christ has made all of this possible for you" (1:12).

Note the phrase, "the Lord Jesus Christ." In ancient times a name represented the presence and person of an individual. When we use the name of Jesus we are speaking of his character, who and what he is. When we glorify the name of our Lord Jesus Christ, we are magnifying him.

Christ will be praised "because of the results they see in you." Is Jesus Christ glorified in us every day that we live? Is he glorified in the way we work, the way we relate to our families, our parents, our husbands and wives, our children? Is he glorified in us in the way we sing, the way we teach, the way we visit? Is he glorified in us in the way we dress, the way we speak, the habits that we have? The praise that God wants from us is the praise that emanates from lives that reveal him.

The trouble with many Christians is that they have the shades pulled down and the doors shut, so the glory and light of Christ is unable to shine in and through them.

Most people are not interested in what they can read in

the Bible or hear from the pulpit. But they are interested in what they can see in us. We are their gospel and their Bible. The way we live and act, the things that we do are preaching the gospel whether we like it or not. Witnessing is neither command, nor option; it is inevitable. The only question is, will we do it to the glory of God or will we bring reproach to the name of God?

The other side of it is, "you belong to him." He belongs to us and we belong to him. It is a beautiful partnership. This is a call away from mediocrity, away from compromise. It is a call to stand and say, "I belong to Christ."

How is all of this going to happen? "The tender mercy of our God and of the Lord Jesus Christ has made all this possible for you." We can do our best, but when we stand before God we will know that every good thing that happened was because of his grace.

What a marvelous Christ we have. How patient he is with us. He calls us and then enables us to be what the call demands of us. What a wonderful opportunity a man has to rise above the level of his own mediocrity and selfishness and to experience eternal joy and happiness in a very personal way in this life.

All of the power of God waits to be unleashed in us to fulfill everything good and to bring praise and glory to our Lord Jesus Christ.

The Great Apostasy
Second Thessalonians 2:1-3a

"And now, what about the coming again of our Lord Jesus Christ, and our being gathered together to meet him? Please don't be upset and excited, dear brothers, by the rumor that this day of the Lord has already begun. If you hear of people having visions and special messages from God about this, or letters that are supposed to have come from me, don't believe them. Don't be carried away and deceived regardless of what they say" (2:1-3).

Second Thessalonians 2 deals with what has been called the great apostasy, the great falling away. This refers to the time when those who had claimed the name of Christ, those who had been a part of the Christian community in their behavior and in their allegiance as far as could be publicly seen, will fall away and disregard the Word of God.

FELLOWSHIP
"Now we beseech you, brethren..." (2:1, KJV). Paul uses the word "brethren" over and over again. The word

means "from the same origin." It speaks of our Christian love for each other and our relationship. "Beseech" means to encourage and to challenge, to lift the heart and bless the soul.

Paul is about to discuss the time when some within the framework of the church are going to quit the church and deny the faith. He is saying that our fellowship as brethren is especially important considering that a great defection is coming. There may come a time when we will be hard-pressed to find anyone that will support us or encourage us. It behooves us to make full use of all that we share in Christ now.

If there was ever a group of people that should stick together, it is God's people. Satan is ecstatic when he can pull us apart, when he can divide us, when he can get us to argue about things that are insignificant and unimportant.

Our Christian fellowship will continue until the coming of the Lord. "We beseech you, brethren, by the coming of the Lord Jesus Christ, and by our gathering together unto him" (2:1, KJV). In the original language there is a single article that ties both of these phrases together, indicating that they belong together. When the Lord comes again, we will be gathered together. It all happens at the same time.

The emphasis here is upon the fact that we will be with him. It is not just that we will be together, but that we will forever be with the Lord. It is the fulfillment of what Paul wrote in 1 Thessalonians 4:17—that living and dead believers will all meet the Lord in the air.

We have beautiful fellowship in him, and it is exciting

to know that the ties we begin now will last throughout all time and all eternity. The relationships we enjoy together now, the bonds that bind our hearts together in Christ now, the love that God gives to us for each other —are all eternal. This fellowship is unaffected by the circumstances of life. If we cannot get happy about fellowship like that, something is wrong with us.

FRUSTRATION
"Please don't be upset and excited" (2:2). Christians should not be shaken and distraught. "Upset" comes from a word used to describe the violent tossing of the waves in a storm, and so expresses tremendous instability and violent upheaval.

"Excited" means to worry. It is in the present tense, which gives the idea of sudden stirring, sudden violent moving of the mind, a continual attitude of discouragement and worry. God did not intend for us to live like that. We must not be victimized by Satan. We must not be shaken in our minds, living in a constant spirit of depression, fear, and frustration.

Apparently some in Thessalonica had had their minds and faith shaken. How did this happen? "If you hear of people having visions and special messages from God about this, or letters that are supposed to have come from me, don't believe them" (2:2). Evidently, as soon as Paul left there was an abundance of interpreters of what he had said. Some even claimed to have fresh revelation from the Spirit of God. "What Paul meant to say was that the day of the Lord has already come," they stated falsely. "Already begun" literally means to be present or to have already occurred.

Some claimed, on authority of special revelation, that the day of the Lord was past. Others tried to deceive the church by saying that the Apostle Paul wrote them a special letter to elaborate on the subject, or claimed to have had a conversation with Paul after he preached his last sermon. There was tremendous confusion on all this.

How do we avoid confusion in the church? By sticking with the Word! The Thessalonians did not have the benefit of a completed Bible, so the Apostle Paul had to write a letter to them which is now part of the Word of God. How do we face those who claim special revelation from the Lord? We must lay that revelation beside the Word of God. Our opinion does not mean much, but God's Word is of eternal importance.

God did not stutter when he gave us his Word. If we will study and read the Word of God and base our lives upon it, then we can know that God is going to bless us as a result of it. Anything that comes into our lives that violates the Word of God will end in frustration and confusion. When God says something, it is so!

Paul refers to "the day of the Lord." The "day of the Lord" is for the world. The "day of Christ," the rapture, is for the church. The day of the Lord is the judgment day of the world when Christ comes with (not for) his saints to punish evil.

These Thessalonian saints had been told that the Lord was going to come back and they would ever be with the Lord. But false teachers said the day of the Lord had already come and God's judgment had already fallen. We can imagine their frustration. They thought they had been left behind. Now Paul writes to declare the truth.

THE FALLING

Before the day of the Lord can come, there must be a great falling away, "a time of great rebellion against God" (2:3). We have here a description of this falling away or apostasy.

"Don't be carried away and deceived regardless of what they say." Satan always has an ambassador ready to deceive us. Working in cooperation with that fact is another—that we are easily deceived, we are gullible.

If we are to avoid being deceived, we must delve heavily into the Word of God. We must pull the Word of God into our hearts, commit it to memory, study it with great discipline. Without the Word of God, we will be deceived—by emotions, friends, Satan, and even coworkers.

"Great rebellion" is the word *apostasia* and is very difficult to interpret. We get our word "apostasy" from it. It means a rebellion or defection. It is "a falling away" (KJV) or "great rebellion." It was used in the Greek language and literature to refer to a military or political rebellion. But the root word has as one of its meanings "a going away."

There are some who think that this falling away, this rebellion, is the rapture of the church, when the church is taken away from the world. Then the man of sin will be revealed. I believe that this is true, but not primarily from this verse. We must stick to the basic meaning of this word, which is a falling away or rebellion. The return of Christ with his saints for judgment upon the earth will not occur until there is a defection. It is almost universally accepted among scholars that this falling away will be within the church. There is going to come a time when church people and churches are going to turn away from God. We are already beginning to see that. Whole segments of the church community are rejecting God. Groups are spurning the principles of the Word of God, and yet still calling themselves the church. If we meet one of the followers of Rev. Moon's Unification Church or of some of the other recent excursions into theological absurdity, we will find that they use Christian language. They will talk about being born again and about salvation, but they have their own definitions. Their teachings give no credence to the Word of God as the final authority. There is already, in the name of Christianity, a falling away.

This is not surprising. John warned that there were already many antichrists (1 John 2:18). "Antichrists" means those who are against Christ, those who turn away from Christ.

Paul declares that there will come a falling away, and we are now seeing a turning away from the things of God. Either we are making progress toward God or we are going away from him. If we are not serving God, we are contributing to a general spirit of rebellion that will ultimately lead to the great apostasy.

SECOND THESSALONIANS 2:1-3a

That does not mean that we who are saved will be lost. First John 2:19 clearly says these who have turned away from God went out from the church so that they might be revealed as not saved, for if they had been saved they would have continued with the church.

By our failure to take a stand for Jesus Christ and to commit ourselves to him, we are contributing to the apostasy of this age. The negligent, carnal Christian is a tool of Satan.

In some of these new religions, the members mortgage their houses and give it all to their "church." They put the titles to their automobiles in the name of the "church." They sell themselves totally to the "church." Yet we genuine believers in Christ have such a complacent attitude toward our faith. If it rains, we find it easy to stay home from public worship. If we have any money left over, then we contribute to Christian causes. Anyone who refuses to sell out totally to Jesus is contributing to a spirit that will result in the great apostasy. The day of the Lord will come and there will be a great falling away. Let us not contribute to it by our negligence.

The Antichrist
Second Thessalonians 2:3b-10

When this great apostasy or rebellion occurs, a great evil personality will take power. He is called by various names, most frequently the Antichrist. There are many antichrists, many who are against Christ, but there will come in the end of the age one worse than all, *the* Antichrist. He will be the personification of evil, everything that Satan wants him to be. This man will be totally dominated and controlled by Satan. We are introduced to him in the third verse of this chapter.

"Don't be carried away and deceived regardless of what they say. For that day will not come until two things happen: first, there will be a time of great rebellion against God, and then the man of rebellion will come —the son of hell." The word "rebellion" is the Greek word for lawlessness, and this is a description of his character. He is a man in rebellion against God. He is not called the man of lawlessness because he is ignorant of God's law, but because he refuses to abide by it.

He is also called the "son of perdition" (KJV). Jesus referred to Judas as the son of perdition. This refers to the final Judas. He has not yet appeared on the scene, because we are dealing with something that has not yet occurred. When this great falling away occurs, *then* this man will be revealed.

The title "son of perdition" or "son of hell" makes it very clear that Antichrist is a lost man. He is not a Christian who becomes rebellious against God. He is an unbeliever doomed to eternal separation from God.

Not only that, he "opposeth and exalteth himself above all that is called God, or that is worshipped" (2:4, KJV). "He will defy every god there is, and tear down every other object of adoration and worship. He will go in and sit as God in the temple of God, claiming that he himself is God. Don't you remember that I told you this when I was with you?" (2:4, 5). He tries to rival God and calls himself God.

The prophet Daniel talked about such a person when he said, "The king will do exactly as he pleases, claiming to be greater than every god there is, even blaspheming the God of gods, and prospering—until his time is up. For God's plans are unshakable. He will have no regard for the gods of his fathers, nor for the god beloved of women, nor any other god, for he will boast that he is greater than them all" (Dan. 11:36, 37). He is going to be a man who wages open hostility against God and has arrogant pride, even claiming to be God.

THE SOVEREIGNTY OF GOD
"And you know what is keeping him from being here already; for he can come only when his time is ready. As

for the work this man of rebellion and hell will do when he comes, it is already going on, but he himself will not come until the one who is holding him back steps out of the way. Then this wicked one will appear, whom the Lord Jesus will burn up with the breath of his mouth and destroy by his presence when he returns. This man of sin will come as Satan's tool, full of satanic power, and will trick everyone with strange demonstrations, and will do great miracles. He will completely fool those who are on their way to hell because they have said 'no' to the Truth; they have refused to believe it and love it, and let it save them" (2:6-10).

Clearly there is someone holding back the evil one, restraining him, keeping him from making his appearance. The Antichrist cannot make his appearance until that which is holding him back is removed.

As wicked and vile as this earth is today, God's sovereignty is still in operation. God's sovereignty is restraining the unbridled attack of Satan upon this world. Were it not for the restraint of God holding him back, there would be such agony, anguish, and despair that we could scarcely talk about it.

"What is keeping him" is a neuter participle in the Greek language. It refers to a power or influence that is holding back the evil one.

In verse 7 Paul says, "the one who is holding him back." That is a masculine participle. In verse 6 Paul says that there is a *power* keeping this man from being revealed, but in verse 7 he says there is a *person* who is keeping this from happening. Some people have been very distressed by this. Some scholars say this spirit of lawlessness or rebellion against all that is right and good is being restrained by the government. As long as there is a government or a power in the land politically, the lawless one cannot be revealed. That is absurd because it is so vague and so general that it could not possibly have had any great consolation to the Thessalonians.

"What is keeping him from being here already" and "the one who is holding him back" is the Holy Spirit. How can the Holy Spirit be described with a neuter participle in one verse and a masculine participle in another? Suppose I were to walk into the room and you were doing something that you should not. Without laying a hand on you, my very presence could restrain you from whatever you were doing. But suppose you were beating your wife and I walked into the room, grabbed your arm, and stopped you from doing it. Presence is one thing, personal involvement another. It would not be unusual to talk about my presence as an "it," but activity is more personal.

The same thing is true of the Holy Spirit. While the Holy Spirit is in the world, his very presence is a restraining factor, keeping evil from reaching its full destructive force. There are other times when the Holy Spirit personally intervenes, not only by his presence in the world but in actual moving in lives to restrain and restrict.

Notice this: the Antichrist, as powerful as he is, as terrible as he is, can do nothing until God allows him to do it. God is still sovereign.

"For he can only come when his time is ready." There

is a time appointed when God is going to take the church away, when the Holy Spirit is going to snatch the bride of Christ out of the world. At that appointed time, the Antichrist will be revealed in all of his awesome, destructive power. But it will not happen one second before God says so. God is sovereign. This cannot come to pass until God allows it.

"The work... is already going on" (2:7). The King James Version says, "The mystery of iniquity doth already work." "Mystery" is the same word used to refer to the gospel in some places in the New Testament. The gospel was once hidden, but now the mystery has been revealed. In the Christian era God revealed the gospel in all its glory and majesty.

The same word is used here concerning the activity of Satan and the Antichrist. The mystery of Satan, the mystery of the Antichrist is already working. There are many secret and mysterious workings of sin. We Christians may be lazy, undisciplined, and uncommitted, but we better realize that while we are moving casually through this life the mystery of iniquity is working day and night. It is not on the surface where everyone can see it, yet. But what we see is just the tip of the iceberg. What we see is just the activity the Holy Spirit has allowed to surface in this world. He has allowed it to surface to call Christians to greater commitment. How sad it is when we see the surfacing of iniquity and rather than being repulsed and driven back to God, we embrace it and thus become part of the mystery of iniquity.

Verse 7 is one of the reasons why I do not believe the

church will go through the tribulation. The Holy Spirit is going to be taken out of the world, and the presence of the Holy Spirit cannot be removed from the earth unless he takes us with him. He lives with us, he abides in us, he dwells in us. The word "dwell" in the New Testament is one which means to make a permanent home. If he has made a permanent home in my life, I cannot be on earth when he is not. When God takes the church out of this world, it will be the removal of restraint, allowing the full revelation of the Antichrist.

THE SERVANT OF SATAN
The Antichrist will be the servant of Satan once the church is gone and the Holy Spirit is removed. "Then this wicked one will appear, whom the Lord Jesus will burn up with the breath of his mouth and destroy by his presence when he returns. This man of sin will come as Satan's tool, full of satanic power, and will do great miracles. He will completely fool those who are on their way to hell because they have said 'no' to the Truth; they have refused to believe it and love it, and let it save them" (2:8-10).

"Appear" means an uncovering, an unveiling, or a revelation. Without question he is going to be a world political figure. I do not believe that the full viciousness, the full vulgarity, the full depth of evil has been revealed in any one person yet. When we have thought of the most vile, vicious, wicked person we could imagine, we still have not come close to describing the Antichrist. He may be on the scene at some point in our lifetime, but he will not be revealed until the Holy Spirit is taken away and the church with him.

This world figure "will come" (2:9) publicly. That word "will come" is *parousia*, the same word used for the return of Christ. Just as Christ is going to come again, the Antichrist is going to come. Jesus is going to come in splendor and power, and so will the Antichrist.

His coming is "as Satan's tool." The Greek word in that phrase is the word for energy. His whole strength, his whole energy, his whole mind, everything that he is will be energized by Satan.

Paul mentions three things that Satan will do in the Antichrist. It is interesting that these same three words are also used to describe the miracles of Jesus. Everything that Jesus is for God, this false christ is for Satan and for evil.

He will have "power" (2:9). "Power" is the word from which we get our word dynamite. He will have a great display of power. "Strange demonstrations" mean that there will be supernatural deeds he will perform to attract attention to himself. "Great miracles" is translated in the King James Version as "lying wonders." The word "wonder" means that he will perform deeds that will absolutely defy the comprehension of man. Paul ties that word with "*pseudos*," false. How could a wonder be a false wonder? Because it is meant to reveal this man as God, but he is not God. It is something that Satan will use to deceive. The Antichrist will appear to be God, the savior of the world. He will seem to have the key to all the economic and social problems of the world. But all his claims are lies.

The first part of the tenth verse declares, "He will completely fool those who are on their way to hell." Hebrews 3:13 talks about our hearts being hardened through the deceitfulness of sin. If we could only learn that sin is not what it seems to be. Satan tells us that we can do this or that and get away with it. He tells us that we can sin and not be hurt. But the truth still stands: the wages of sin is death. There is no escape from that. Do not be deceived. What we sow, we will reap.

The whole program of Satan is to deceive us and to misrepresent the truth. If we would believe God just half as much as we believe Satan, there would be no lack of faith for any of us. Satan is contrary to everything we believe; yet we fall to his lies. If we have someone leading our business into bankruptcy, we fire him. If a manager of a baseball team cannot win ballgames, we get rid of him. Satan is an eternal loser, and yet we blindly follow him. Let us beware of his deceptions.

By this time the church of Thessalonica was probably wondering if they could possibly face someone like this Antichrist. It is important to see what is going to happen to this servant of Satan. "Whom the Lord Jesus will burn up with the breath of his mouth and destroy by his presence" (2:8). "Burn up" tells us what is going to happen to the Antichrist personally. "Destroy" refers to what is going to happen to all of his plans, his program, everything he intends to do.

The Antichrist will be burned up "with the breath of

his [Christ's] mouth." The devil's man is going to flex his muscles, do all these wonderful signs, set himself up as God, and prepare to fight the Lord. But it will be no contest. The Lord will just say, "Be gone" and that will be the end. Just one word from God's mouth will defeat the Antichrist.

That is a consistent teaching of the Word of God. In Revelation we read that as the struggle of the end comes and the Antichrist marshals all of his forces, "the remnant were slain with the sword of him that sat upon the horse, which sword proceeded out of his mouth" (Rev. 19:21, KJV). Isaiah 11:4 and Job 4:9 also speak of the wicked being consumed by a word from God.

Jesus Christ will destroy all of the Antichrist's plans with the brightness of his coming. By just making his appearance, Jesus will wipe out the Antichrist. What optimism this creates for us!

The world is moving toward a climax when evil will make its last stand, but Satan's plan will be aborted by our God.

THE STATE OF SINNERS
The Antichrist will "completely fool those who are on their way to hell" (2:10). Why are they going to hell? Because "they have said 'no' to the Truth; they have refused to believe it."

Those who are separated from God and so are lost are on their way to hell. It may not appear that way in this life. Here it may seem that evil is triumphing, as though people who are bad come out on top. But the Bible declares that they are perishing, they are dying. If one does not know Jesus Christ as his personal Savior, regardless of how many churches he belongs to or how honest he may be or how hard-working and diligent he may be, he is perishing, he is doomed. Furthermore, if one is not a servant of Jesus Christ, he is a servant of the Antichrist. We are against Christ or we are for him. We cannot be neutral. We cannot decide later. Refusal to decide now is to choose against him.

"They have said 'no' to the Truth; they have refused to believe it." They do not go to hell because they do not know the truth, but because they rejected it. They do not go into eternal punishment because they do not understand, but because they refuse to understand. If a man is separated from God today, it is not God's fault, but his own. God has made every possible attempt to draw us to himself.

It is inconceivable that anyone would choose death rather than life, darkness rather than light, unhappiness rather than peace and happiness. But people all over this world today are making that choice. They are perishing, not by God's decree but by their own decision.

25
Believing a Lie
Second Thessalonians 2:11, 12

"So God will allow them to believe lies with all their hearts, and all of them will be justly judged for believing falsehood, refusing the Truth, and enjoying their sins" (2:11, 12). These verses are written out of the backdrop of rejection of Christ. They refused to accept the gospel. They refused to believe that Christ was the Messiah. They would not accept what God had said.

THE GREAT REJECTION
Verse 11 begins with the word "so," meaning "because of what has been said." The King James Version says, "For this cause." Because men rejected God and refused to respond to his claims, they will be greatly deceived. God is able to do only what we allow him to do as it relates to our salvation. God does not overrule man's choice. God has created us with a free will. Circumstances and pressures influence our choices, but ultimately we make the decisions that we want to make. God will never override man's choice.

Believing a Lie

To a great degree, everything God would do in our lives is dependent on our response to his truth. If we push God's truth out of our lives, if we refuse to respond to his claims and to love his truth, it limits what God is able to do in our lives. If we say no to God, God will leave us with our choice. He never forces his way into anyone's experience, but always comes only by invitation. "Look! I have been standing at the door and I am constantly knocking. If anyone hears me calling him and opens the door, I will come in and fellowship with him and he with me" (Rev. 3:20).

No man will ever be saved until he chooses to be saved. We will never grow in God's grace until we allow God the liberty to grow through us and to lead us on to maturity.

THE GREAT DECEPTION

"God will allow them to believe lies." The King James Version says, "God shall send them strong delusion." Some say there is a moral law in the universe because of which we must reap the results of our sinfulness. The Bible does not say that. Punishment of sin is inevitable, not because of the moral laws of the universe, but because there is a personal God who says, "I will see to it that you will be punished."

"Strong delusion" is literally "energy of error." The word "energy" or "energizing" has been seen in several places in previous passages. We have seen the energy of Satan, the working of Satan, and the mystery of iniquity.

"Energy of falsehood or error" means that God is going to spark or encourage man's rejection.

We may think that doesn't sound right, but God never overrules our decision. If we establish a pattern of rejection against God, that rejection will cause further rejection against God. And God will not force us away from that pattern.

Five times Exodus declares that Pharaoh hardened his heart. Later it says that God hardened Pharaoh's heart. What happened was that God let Pharaoh do what he really wanted to do. God allowed him to continue in his rebellion. God hardened Pharaoh's heart, but this was in keeping with what had already been determined by Pharaoh.

The first chapter of Romans speaks over and over again of the great rebellion of men against God. Professing themselves to be wise, they became fools. They did not glorify God, but were vain in their imagination. They were ungrateful. They changed the glory of a holy God into the image of beasts. "Wherefore God also gave them up to uncleanness, through the lusts of their own hearts" (Rom. 1:24, KJV). God simply gave them over to a reprobate mind and allowed them to receive in themselves the results of their error.

The punishment of sin is for us to get what sin pays. God allows us to go on in sin and enjoy our sins until we finally realize that the path we have chosen is nothing less than hell on earth. We choose sin for our lives and God will allow that sin to destroy us.

"God will allow them to believe lies." It literally says they will believe "the lie," referring to the Antichrist.

The Antichrist will say he is God, and people who are used to going along with evil and who are determined that God will have no place in their lives will believe him.

THE GREAT RETRIBUTION

"And all of them will be justly judged for believing falsehood, refusing the Truth, and enjoying their sins" (2:12). The words translated "justly judged" come from a word which does not speak of consequences as much as the judicial process of God. Paul is declaring that we never get away with our sin. Not only does this word imply that God will bring punishment upon us, but it specifically says God will judge us. God does not wink at sin. He cannot pretend that it is not there. He will judge it. Those who rebel against God can be sure that the God who allowed their rebellion to continue will pass judgment upon them. This is a reference to the final judgment.

If we really understood this, it would make a great deal of difference in the way we live. Down deep inside, we think we can promise God anything and he will accept it and leave us alone. We feel we can do what we want to, abide by the principles we choose, live the way we want to live. But God will judge us.

This truth is not designed to frighten us, but to remind us of the real values of life, to remind us that life is not all fun and games and we cannot live as we please.

God did not create us merely for this life. He did not create this magnificent mechanism of the human body and soul simply to exist for a few years upon this earth, to be bound and hounded by sin, and ultimately the grave. That is not the whole story. God created us for perfect fellowship with him. He gave us this life to determine where we would spend eternity, whether with him or separated from him.

God is saying to us, "Be careful what you do. Do not establish a pattern that will ultimately lead you into deep rebellion against God."

THE GREAT DETERIORATION
"All of them will be justly judged for believing falsehood, refusing the Truth, and enjoying their sins." This may start off innocently enough. "I wonder if God really means what he says. I don't really believe he does." But disbelief in God never ends with innocent doubt. First they believed what was false, but they wound up "enjoying their sins." There was disbelief of God, then delight in sin.

Our conscience can be seared, no longer sensing right and wrong, no longer sensitive to spiritual things. We then go on sinning not because our circumstances prompt us to sin, but because we like it. It delights us.

Every time we disbelieve God, we take another step toward that ultimate deterioration of character that causes us to delight in doing evil. That is exactly the way the first chapter of Romans ends. "Who, knowing the judgment of God, that they which commit such things are worthy of death, not only do the same, but have pleasure in them that do them" (Rom. 1:32, KJV).

Here is a person who likes to steal. It started out innocently enough, maybe stealing a candy bar from a grocery store, or cheating on exams. It was just a little thing at first. Or here is a man who cheats on his wife, or a wife who cheats on her husband. Or here is someone who is dishonest on his income tax. At first, it seemed necessary, but now they enjoy it. They like the romance, the intrigue. They want to see if they can get away with it.

The same thing is true of some who lie. They started off telling lies to cover up something. They got so good at it that now they tell lies just for the sake of telling lies. They will fib about what time they got off work, where they went, etc. They lie because they like to lie.

God is saying here that when we take the first step of rebellion against him, we need to repent of it and commit it to God immediately so this delusion can't continue in our lives.

Few people ever intend to end up in deep sin. But we are easily deceived in our sinfulness. For example, there are thousands of people in our churches who believe they can be spiritual without reading the Bible. They were told by some of their peers that they were spiritual people, how much blessing they had been to those who know them, etc. Yet they know in their hearts that they do not study the Word or have the devotional time that they should. They begin to believe they can be spiritual without spiritual discipline.

Notice the pattern here. First, they simply did not receive the love of the truth (2:10). That sounds innocent enough. But now Paul says they do not believe it at all

(2:11, 12). If we do not receive the truth, we will find ourselves opposing it. There was no warmth for the gospel in their hearts, and so there came warmth for evil. We will serve God or Satan. Which side are we on?

There is a contrast in verse 11 between sin and truth. They believed not the truth; they had pleasure in sin. Either we welcome God's truth or we enjoy sin. There is no other alternative.

It is about time for us as God's people to decide which side we are on, to get off the fence. If we are not serving God, then we are moving toward a time when we will with pleasure and delight serve Satan. The very anguish and pangs of hell will fasten itself on us if we make such a choice.

That would be like a man who hits his finger with a hammer. It hurts, but he keeps striking it until at last it is numb and he doesn't feel the pain, so he continues his foolish behavior.

When I take one step away from God, it becomes easier to take the second step. One may say, "I am going to be honest when I get through this exam," but he has begun a direction of dishonesty that can ultimately climax in tragedy for his life. Every time we reject the truth of God, it becomes easier for us to do it again.

Sometimes we find ourselves having to say, "I never thought this would happen to me, to my family, to my church." If we trace it back, we find that it all began because somewhere down the line we took a step away from God. Dedication was replaced by compromise. Ultimately we believed a lie and began to delight in our sin.

Called
by the
Gospel
*Second
Thessalonians
2:13, 14*

These verses are especially important because they give a comprehensive picture of our salvation through Christ.

"But we must forever give thanks to God for you, our brothers loved by the Lord, because God chose from the very first to give you salvation, cleansing you by the work of the Holy Spirit and by your trusting in the Truth. Through us he told you the Good News. Through us he called you to share in the glory of our Lord Jesus Christ" (2:13, 14).

The very first word is a conjunction, showing contrast. Paul has just told us about the sad consequences of rebellion against God. As a contrast, he says in effect, "This is not so with you. You have responded to God's grace." The word "must" is a repeat of a phrase that he used earlier in Thessalonians when he spoke about his responsibility to praise these people. He must praise them because of what God had done in them.

Because of the fruit in their lives, it would not be right for him to keep silent about them, nor to keep silent in his prayers to God concerning them. He said, "You have been so consistent, so Christ-like, it would be wrong for me not to thank God for you." He adds the word "forever" to this reminder of his prayers for them. Their lives, day by day, were always so consistent that he had to always be thanking God for them.

Would it not be wonderful if our commitment to Jesus Christ was like that, a commitment that was so consistent, so fruitful, so solid that every day we would be thanking God, gratefully praising God for his work through each other.

Then he says, "Our brothers loved by the Lord." Earlier he called them "dear brothers, much beloved of God" (1 Thess. 1:4). Paul has just finished talking about the mighty power of Satan, the lord of evil, the one who is going to bring all great difficulties and sadness into the world. He has just described the great assault of the evil one upon God's people and the world. Now he says, "You are loved by the Lord." "Lord" is the word for dominion or governing power. The mighty power of evil will be unleashed upon the world, but Christians do not need to worry because they are kept by the Lord. They are protected, guided, and guarded in the love of Jesus Christ. It is wonderful for us to know that in our warfare with evil we do not stand in our own strength, but in his.

THE DIVINE CHOICE
"God chose from the very first to give you salvation, cleansing you by the work of the Holy Spirit and by your trusting in the Truth." Here we are confronted with the reality of the sovereignty of God and divine election.

Here we have laid before us the fact that God in his sovereignty initiated man's salvation. Man is not saved because he wants to be, but because God made the first move. It was God who sought Adam in the garden, and down through the years it has been God who has sought and carefully drawn man to himself. We speak about the time when we "found the Lord," but the truth is the Lord found us.

He says, first of all, that God's choice was no afterthought. God made it from the very first. What "very first" is he talking about? Scholars are divided on this, but I do not see any real reason to deviate from the plain interpretation of other passages in the New Testament. In Ephesians 1:4 and 2 Timothy 1:9, this idea means before the world as we know it.

"He chose to give you salvation" (2:13). Here is one of the most comprehensive descriptions of salvation anywhere. These verses point out to us that salvation begins with the new birth, continues with a growing and maturing in moral character, and climaxes in eternal glory with Jesus Christ. Those who are deceived and rebel against God will receive damnation. But those who respond to the claims of God will receive salvation.

When we come to the matter of divine choice, we come to one of the most controversial subjects to be found anywhere in the Word of God. What does the Word of God say about this matter of God's election?

Remember that we can get into real trouble if we try to isolate verses of Scripture. Ultrapredestinarians base their views on statements such as, "God hath from the beginning chosen you to salvation" (2:13, KJV). How-

*Called
by the Gospel*

ever, there is no period there in the original language or in the thought of the verses. Paul continues, "cleansing you by..." or "by means of." How is a man elected for salvation? It is done by means of two things: by the cleansing work of the Holy Spirit and by trusting in the Truth.

God initiates salvation, but God's choice is always accompanied by man's choice. We are saved when God's Holy Spirit works transforming miracles in our lives, but he never works in our lives unless we believe. The two matters go hand in hand.

"For from the very beginning God decided that those who came to him—and all along he knew who would—should become like his Son, so that his Son would be the First, with many brothers. And having chosen us, he called us to come to him; and when we came, he declared us 'not guilty,' filled us with Christ's goodness, gave us right standing with himself, and promised us his glory" (Rom. 8:29, 30). It all starts off with the foreknowledge of God. God's choosing is based on his knowledge of who is going to respond.

Faith joins us with God. "If you tell others with your own mouth that Jesus Christ is your Lord, and believe in your heart that God has raised him from the dead, you will be saved. For it is by believing in his heart that a man becomes right with God; and with his mouth he tells others of his faith, confirming his salvation.... Anyone who calls upon the name of the Lord will be saved" (Rom. 10:9, 10, 13).

If man is not free to respond to the choice of God, then life is a charade and God is a devilish fiend who delights in torturing man. The conclusion of those who overstress the doctrine of predestination and election is: no evangelism, no witnessing, no missions. Biblically, God seeks and draws, but man can stay lost. Man can decide to reject the salvation offered by a sovereign God.

We could not worship a God who would be so fiendish as to draw a man but not let him have the capacity to say yes. Being able to say yes also means being able to say no. That is free will. Man has a choice and God has a choice. Salvation occurs when man's choice coincides with God's choice.

If we will study carefully the eighth through the eleventh chapters of the book of Romans, we will find the free will of man and the sovereignty of God both emphasized very strongly. If we read only certain passages, we may say that man is completely free. If we read other portions, we may think God is completely sovereign, that his election is absolutely arbitrary and man has no choice. What are we to do? We must simply believe what God says: man has free will to respond to the will of God; and God is sovereign. If man is not free to choose, witnessing is a game. If God is not sovereign, salvation is of man. We reject neither free will or sovereignty, but embrace both.

The best conclusion is this: "Oh, what a wonderful God we have! How great are his wisdom and knowledge and riches! How impossible it is for us to understand his decisions and his methods! For who among us can know the mind of the Lord? Who knows enough to be his counselor and guide? And who could ever offer to the Lord enough to induce him to act? For everything comes from

God alone. Everything lives by his power, and everything is for his glory. To him be glory evermore" (Rom. 11:33-36).

If we try to figure it out with our minds, we cannot do it. There are many things about Christianity that we cannot intellectually reconcile. We accept the election and sovereignty of God by faith just as we do everything else that is dear to our faith. We cannot understand the Bible on these deep matters intellectually. We cannot understand how the death of a man 2,000 years ago could bring salvation to us today, but we know it does. We cannot intellectually accept the virgin birth of Christ. It is illogical, but by faith we accept it. We cannot intellectually accept the Trinity. We accept it by faith.

We are responsible to God. God's sovereignty does not relieve us of our responsibility to respond to him. God's choice does not make it unnecessary for us to choose. That is why we preach. That is why we teach. That is why we visit. That is why we invite people to come to God.

Charles Spurgeon described it best: "Over the door to salvation is a sign and as you approach the door, it says, 'Whosoever will, let him take the water of life freely.' The man receives Christ and walks through the door. As he walks through, he turns and looks back at the door which says, 'Foreordained from before the foundations of the world.' " That is about as good an explanation as I can find. "Whosoever will" is man's part. "Foreordained" is God's part. We pervert the gospel if we accept one and discard the other.

SECOND
THESSALONIANS 2:13, 14

THE HUMAN CHOICE
No man is saved until the transforming power of the Holy Spirit is unleashed in him. No man grows in God unless the Holy Spirit moves him to maturity. That work of the Holy Spirit is always accomplished through our belief in the Truth.

"Through us he called you to share in the glory of our Lord Jesus Christ" (2:14). God chose the Thessalonians, and the Holy Spirit saved them through the gospel that was preached to them by Paul. We share in the sovereign grace of God as we proclaim the gospel of Jesus Christ.

There is a beautiful passage in Romans concerning this: "Anyone who calls upon the name of the Lord will be saved. But how shall they ask him to save them unless they believe in him? And how can they believe in him if they have never heard about him? And how can they hear about him unless someone tells them? And how will anyone go and tell them unless someone sends him? That is what the Scriptures are talking about when they say, 'How beautiful are the feet of those who preach the Gospel of peace with God and bring glad tidings of good things.' In other words, how welcome are those who come preaching God's Good News!" (Rom. 10:13-15).

The greatest privilege and joy in the world is that of preaching the gospel, of sharing the good news of Jesus Christ. Something is wrong with us if we are not excited about the opportunity that God has given to us to be a part of his redemptive purposes.

This church in Thessalonica was born through preaching. Paul and his associates were only there from a few weeks to a few months, but as a result a church began. The Book of Acts declares that when persecution came, the Christians were scattered abroad. Everywhere they went they preached the Word. They shared Jesus Christ. That must be our purpose too. God has placed us in the world to be lighthouses pointing men to God.

There is no growth and maturity without witnessing and sharing our faith. God did not give us the gospel to be used as a personal fire escape. "When someone becomes a Christian he becomes a brand new person inside. He is not the same any more. A new life has begun! All these new things are from God who brought us back to himself through what Christ Jesus did. And God has given us the privilege of urging everyone to come into his favor and be reconciled to him. For God was in Christ, restoring the world to himself, no longer counting men's sins against them but blotting them out. This is the wonderful message he has given us to tell others. We are Christ's ambassadors. God is using us to speak to you: we beg you, as though Christ himself were here pleading with you, receive the love he offers you —be reconciled to God" (2 Cor. 5:17-20).

The climax of all this is "the glory of our Lord Jesus Christ." Those who have been redeemed by Christ will share his glory. Many people think that if they get saved they will lose all the happiness of life. That is the opposite of the truth. Everything that is worthwhile in life is found through Jesus Christ. Every worthy ambition of our souls is fulfilled in him. That desire to be important, to be somebody, to achieve will never find its fulfillment except in Jesus Christ. Jesus gave importance and value to the individual. The gospel of Christ elevated man to his highest level of dignity. Everything our hearts long to experience, we discover through Jesus Christ.

Then he takes us on into eternity, to share his glory forever. That makes it all worthwhile. That turmoil we wish we could get rid of, Jesus will get rid of it for us. That confusion we pray could somehow be removed, Jesus will remove it. He will give us peace and life, starting now. And he will take us through death to share his glory. Hallelujah!

Standing Tall for God
Second Thessalonians 2:15-17

These verses reveal much to us about Christian pilgrimage. The Christian is not to dream, but to fight. The Christian is called not to stand still, but to climb upward. The Christian is not only called to a great privilege, though it is a privilege to be a Christian and to serve God, but to a tremendous task.

"With all these things in mind, dear brothers, stand firm and keep a strong grip on the truth that we taught you in our letters and during the time we were with you. May our Lord Jesus Christ himself and God our Father, who has loved us and given us everlasting comfort and hope which we don't deserve, comfort your hearts with all comfort, and help you in every good thing you say and do" (2:15-17).

One thing this passage reveals is that divine grace does not exclude human activity. We are saved by grace; yet we are created anew in Christ Jesus for good works (Eph. 2:10). So, while we are saved by an act of divine grace, there rests upon us certain duties and obligations. Salvation not only brings forgiveness for eternity, but a purpose for time.

INSTRUCTION
"Stand firm" and "keep a strong grip" (2:15) are present imperatives. The idea is that we are to hold to these truths and to keep holding to them. We are to stand against error and against wrong by standing for God and for truth. "Stand tall for God," he is saying. "Stand firm for God."

"Keep a strong grip" is from a word used many times for the grip of the hand. Paul is declaring, "You have had the gospel presented to you, now hold on to it." It is a reminder to us of the constancy and steadfastness we should have toward the gospel.

The word "truth" (2:15) refers to the gospel that had been preached by the Apostle Paul. This refers particularly to the truth contained in 1 Thessalonians.

We live in one of the most dangerous days spiritually that has ever dawned. Almost without exception the cult groups that are sweeping across America have some "Christian" base. They claim the Bible as a sacred writing. Many of them claim Jesus Christ as one of their founding prophets or one of the great men of their faith. We face today the most dangerous form of heresy—that which sounds like the truth. It seems to have reason and logic on its side, and yet it deviates from God's path.

The Christian church needs to affirm its uncompromising commitment to the Word of God. The Bible is our road map. We are to hold fast and stand tall upon the doctrine that God has given to us in the gospel.

INTERCESSION
"May our Lord Jesus Christ himself and God our Father, who has loved us and given us everlasting comfort and hope which we don't deserve, comfort your hearts with all comfort, and help you in every good thing you say and do" (2:16, 17). In our own strength we cannot do what God has instructed us to do. The Christian life is not a matter of God saving us and then telling us to do good on our own. The Christian life is God saving us, and then continuing to live his life through us. If we have found ourselves continually beaten down and defeated in our Christian lives, it may be because we have not understood that the Christian life is a life of victory through surrender. God works through us as we are available for his use.

"May our Lord Jesus Christ himself and God our Father...." It is not unusual for God and Christ to be linked together as equals. The unusual thing here is that the name of Jesus is first. That only occurs a couple of other times in the New Testament. In the Greek we have plural subjects and singular verbs, indicating that each subject is given equal value. Jesus and God have equal authority and power. Jesus is God!

The deity of Jesus Christ is the foundation upon which the church is built. "Then he asked them, 'Who do you think I am?' Simon Peter answered, 'The Christ, the

Messiah, the Son of the living God.' 'God has blessed you, Simon, son of Jonah,' Jesus said, 'for my Father in heaven has personally revealed this to you—this is not from any human source. You are Peter, a stone; and upon this rock I will build my church; and all the powers of hell shall not prevail against it' " (Matt. 16:15-18). It is the rock of the deity of Christ that the church is built on. If Jesus Christ is not fully divine, then our worship is a farce.

Since Jesus is divine, he possesses all of the authority and power of God. Thus, what he says is binding upon us. Most professing Christians don't understand this or they would not live the way they live. It makes a great deal of difference in our attitude toward Christ when we realize that when we speak of Christ, we are speaking of God!

Since Christ is God, we had better listen to him. Christianity is not just playing church and being good and honest. It is a matter of obeying the God of the universe. That is why the sternest words in the New Testament are directed to those who attack the person of Christ. The deity of Jesus Christ is the cardinal doctrine and truth of the Word of God. Anyone who denies that is cutting the very heart out of the gospel. To know Jesus is to have the eternal God living through us.

The Savior is "our Lord Jesus Christ." These words speak of majesty and authority. They are words that compel commitment.

God "has loved us and given us..." (2:16). These words are aorist participles in the Greek language, giving it the connotation of something that happened in the past but still has present implication and value. When Paul says that Jesus and the Father have loved us, he is speaking of a definite action that has already taken place and still is taking place. "Loved" doubtless refers back to the cross and to the death of Jesus Christ. Jesus died on the cross because he loved us, and he still loves us.

God has given us "everlasting comfort." "Has given" is past tense, but "everlasting" reaches into the future. The word "comfort" is from the Greek word *parakaleo*, which means to encourage. *Paraklete* is the word used to describe the Holy Spirit and means an encourager or comforter. God and Jesus Christ have already given us everlasting encouragement. We have this now, but it will never end. When we get to glory, God will keep on blessing our lives through this everlasting encouragement. It is exciting to realize that every problem we shall face in the future, every need that we shall encounter in the days ahead, God has already given comfort and encouragement for. Nothing that happens to us is going to surprise God. All we need has been given to us at a point in the past, and continues to be given day by day.

Then Paul declares that we have received "hope which we don't deserve." The King James Version calls it a "good hope." Because God has moved into our lives, no longer is the future dreaded, no longer is life without meaning or purpose. This comes through God's grace.

Every good anticipation and every good hope that ever comes into our hearts is the result of God's grace in our lives. If we want peace and happiness in life, if we want direction, purpose, meaning, we will find it through God's grace in Jesus Christ.

"Comfort your hearts with all comfort" (2:17). This is a picture of shoring up potential weaknesses in our lives, of preparing for what lies ahead. It speaks of vigorous action, brave and courageous endurance.

Paul prays that God will "help you in every good thing you say and do" (2:17). God wants our faith to be demonstrated in our lives. God can strengthen our hearts so that the words we speak and the works we do please him and bless others. The wonderful thing is that if this prayer is fulfilled, it brings honor and praise to God. What God gives, we give back to him. He comforts and establishes us so that what proceeds from our lives will glorify him.

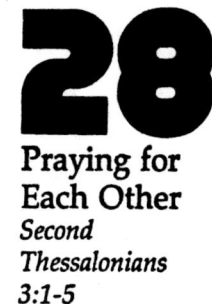

28
Praying for Each Other
Second Thessalonians 3:1-5

"Finally, dear brothers, as I come to the end of this letter I ask you to pray for us. Pray first that the Lord's message will spread rapidly and triumph wherever it goes, winning converts everywhere as it did when it came to you. Pray too that we will be saved out of the clutches of evil men, for not everyone loves the Lord. But the Lord is faithful; he will make you strong and guard you from satanic attacks of every kind. And we trust the Lord that you are putting into practice the things we taught you, and that you always will. May the Lord bring you into an ever deeper understanding of the love of God and of the patience that comes from Christ" (3:1-5).

Paul begins by saying, "Pray for us." How different life could be for us if we devoted our lives to praying for each other. Think for a moment of how much we criticize and complain about each other rather than praying for God's blessings on our hearts.

The Apostle Paul has encouraged these Christians and now he says, "You needed me to present the gospel to you, but I need you now. I need you to pray for me." The tense in the original language—"pray"—is the continuous present tense. He is saying, "We want you to pray for us and keep on praying for us."

GOD'S GLORY

First of all, we are to pray for God's glory. Many times we pray selfishly, but we should "pray first that the Lord's message will spread rapidly and triumph wherever it goes."

Paul often wrote about the Word of *God*, but here he says, "the word of the *Lord*" (KJV). There is a very strong reason for that. He has spent some time discussing the man of sin, the great wicked leader who will oppose God. He uses the term "the Lord" to help these Christians realize that Satan is never going to have the upper hand. Satan will not have the victory. There is opposition to the cause of Christ. We are tempted and oppressed. But in spite of all the opposition, in spite of the approaching man of sin, Jesus is still Lord and he will rule.

"Spread rapidly" (3:1) is an athletic term and gives the idea of a swift, winning race. Paul is saying, "Let us pray that the Word of the Lord will have ready acceptance on the part of those who hear it." Concerning the Word of God, the psalmist declared, "How swiftly his word flies" (Ps. 147:15).

When we respond to the claims of the Word of God it triumphs, or as the King James Version says, it is "glorified." When the world is able to see that God has done a work in our lives, then the Word of God is glorified because it is demonstrated in our lives. God intended that his Word be received gloriously in our hearts and be manifested for all to see.

GOD'S STRENGTH

"Pray too that we will be saved out of the clutches of evil men, for not everyone loves the Lord" (3:2). If we live in our strength we will fail. When we pray, we must not pray, "God, let us be strong." We must pray, "God, strengthen us. Move into our lives. Deliver us, for we cannot deliver ourselves."

So many Christians go through their lives in a tragic cycle of defeat and despair. When we pray, we are to pray admitting to God that we are weak and that we need his strength in our lives. If we are ever to live the Christian life to its fullest, it will be through the power of God working through us.

GOD'S PROVISION

Notice what God will provide when we pray to him: "But the Lord is faithful; he will make you strong and guard you from satanic attacks of every kind. And we trust the Lord that you are putting into practice the things we taught you, and that you always will. May the Lord bring you into an ever deeper understanding of the love of God and of the patience that comes from Christ" (3:3-5).

"The Lord is faithful." That stood in contrast to the

unfaithfulness of the men who were opposing Paul. Not all men love the Lord (3:2). But God is faithful and true. He will keep his word. God is One upon whom we can depend.

The words "make you strong" speak of strengthening the inner man. He will ground us upon the solid foundation. Inwardly, he puts our feet on the solid rock. Outwardly, he will "guard you from satanic attacks of every kind." The original language does not mention Satan, but speaks of "evil," obviously referring to the assault of satanic forces upon our lives. Paul has been speaking about the personal conflict between God and Satan, between the Son of God and the son of lawlessness. So it seems likely that what he is saying here is that when we pray for God's provision, God will guard us and shield us from the evil one. That is good news!

When Jesus said to pray, "Don't bring us into temptation" (Matt. 6:13), he was literally saying, "Don't ever start leading us into temptation." He was declaring that if God ever started to lead us into temptation, we would not make it. God promises to establish us inwardly and to guard us outwardly through our prayers.

In verse 1, Paul asked these converts to "pray for us." Then in verse 3, instead of saying, "God is going to establish me and keep me from evil," he says, "God is going to establish you and keep you from evil." Notice what has happened. Paul started out with a great need for someone to pray for him. But as he sought their prayers for him, his own heart was moved to pray for them. He is requesting God's provision and God's strength and yet he says, "As you pray for me, you will

SECOND THESSALONIANS 3:1-5

receive God's strength and provision." There is a wonderful reciprocal nature to prayer. It is a wonderful thing to see this apostle, burdened by the opposition of hostile men, moved to claim God's very best for those he loved.

"And we trust the Lord that you are putting into practice the things we taught you, and that you always will" (3:4). The phrase "we trust the Lord" is extremely important, because that is the only way that the Christian life can be lived. He didn't say, "We have confidence in you," but rather, "We have confidence in the Lord concerning you." "And I am sure that God who began the good work within you will keep right on helping you grow in his grace until his task within you is finally finished on that day when Jesus Christ returns" (Phil. 1:6). When God starts a work in our lives, he will see it through.

This is the first time the Apostle Paul moves into the future tense. Up until this time, he has praised them for what they have done thus far. But here he expresses his confidence that they "always will" do God's will.

Then Paul issues another prayer. "May the Lord bring you into an ever deeper understanding of the love of God and of the patience that comes from Christ" (3:5). There is the word "Lord" again. Paul uses that title five times in these five verses. We serve a ruling, victorious, conquering Lord. He is not going to leave us at the mercy of evil. He is not going to abandon us. He is victor over sin and evil. May *this* "Lord bring you into an ever deeper understanding." "Bring" is the same Greek word translated "send" in 1 Thessalonians 3:11. It is a word we might use if we were building a road. It means to make the road smooth, make it straight, prepare it. Paul is praying that God will make a road straight from your heart to the love of God and to the patience of Christ.

Some think that "love" here means our love for God. Others say it means God's love for us. It means both. We love him because he first loved us. As we experience the fulfilling and transforming love of God, we love God in return. If we could live in an awareness of God's love, what a difference it would make as we labor and serve.

"Patience" is a word that is used to describe the tenacity of Jesus Christ in going all the way to the cross, and here refers to his patient endurance, his steadfastness in staying in God's will and fulfilling God's plan for his life. When we have been introduced to his steadfastness, we, too, will stay on God's path. Just as he endured, so will we.

As we obey God, he will direct us day by day into a deeper understanding of his love for us, thus calling for a deeper love from us. He will lead us into a deeper experience of the patient endurance and steadfast purpose of Jesus Christ.

29
An Example to Follow
Second Thessalonians 3:6-9

When we come to verse 6 we come to one of the longest single sections of either 1 or 2 Thessalonians. Anything that receives this much attention from the Apostle Paul must be very important for us to consider. The subject? Laziness, busybodies, those who won't work and thus become a burden upon the people of God.

"Now here is a command, dear brothers, given in the name of our Lord Jesus Christ by his authority: Stay away from any Christian who spends his days in laziness and does not follow the ideal of hard work we set up for you. For you well know that you ought to follow our example: you never saw us loafing; we never accepted food from anyone without buying it; we worked hard day and night for the money we needed to live on, in order that we would not be a burden to any of you. It wasn't that we didn't have the right to ask you to feed us, but we wanted to show you, firsthand, how you should work for your living" (3:6-9).

Notice he gives a command to obey. This is no option. This is an imperative. To underscore the authority behind this command, Paul declares that it is "given in the

An Example to Follow

name of our Lord Jesus Christ." This was not just Paul's idea. It carried all of the authority of the Lord Jesus Christ.

The combination of "command" and "dear brothers" shows sternness blended with tenderness. "Dear brothers" is a warm term of Christian fellowship and love. Paul refers to one who has done wrongly as a "brother" (KJV) or "Christian." We ought to follow Paul's example in blending authority with concern.

Apparently the congregation as a whole was doing pretty well. Paul tells them to withdraw from "every brother..." (KJV). "Every brother" is singular, indicating that the majority of the people were sound and healthy in the faith. But a few were failing to live properly, and Paul speaks to the entire church regarding the conduct of those few. Sometimes we feel that if only a few people are stumbling in some wrong, then we should just praise those who are doing well and ignore those who are doing poorly. But one rotten apple can spoil the whole barrel. Relationships within the fellowship of the church need to be closely guarded and carefully examined.

A CAUTIOUS FELLOWSHIP
We are to be very cautious concerning those whose lifestyle is contrary to the cause of Christ. Let's examine the word "laziness" or "disorderly" (KJV) since it is a key word here. It is the same word translated "lazy" in

1 Thessalonians 5:14. The problem in that passage was idleness, the basic root meaning of the word. Paul is talking about the same people in both passages. They had not heeded his first message. This word could also be translated "undisciplined."

"Laziness" refers primarily to physical discipline. Since we have such emphasis on our physical life, consider how much more significant is our need of spiritual discipline. We are often more concerned about whether we weigh too much or how we look than we are about spending enough time with God in prayer and Bible study.

Paul tells us to "stay away from" such undisciplined people. Some think this means to kick them out of the church. However, that is not the intent of the passage because later he says, "Don't think of him as an enemy, but speak to him as you would to a brother" (3:15). He is not saying we should remove our fellowship from him, but that our fellowship with the disorderly needs to be guarded. We must not give intimate fellowship to those who are of this disposition because in the eyes of others we would be condoning their actions and thus appear to agree with them.

Verse 11 refers to "busybodies" (KJV). That word really means meddlesome. These people are always taking care of everybody else's business, meddling in matters that should be none of their concern.

These lazy people were asking the church to support them, expecting the church to provide their livelihood. They reasoned that Jesus was going to come back soon, so why not just live off the church until that time? Also, they were spreading malicious gossip about the second coming (2:2).

There is no place in the service of our Lord for an undisciplined person, one who sets aside "the ideal of hard work we set up for you" (3:6). The great apostle had shown them how to live and work. When you listen to a man preach, look at his life to see if it backs up what he preaches. God requires that what we teach and preach, we ought to walk and live. This requires great discipline.

A CAREFUL "FOLLOWSHIP"

We need to be careful about our fellowship with those who are disorderly, but we need to be just as careful about following the right kind of leaders. "For you well know that you ought to follow our example: you never saw us loafing; we never accepted food from anyone without buying it; we worked hard day and night for the money we needed to live on, in order that we would not be a burden to any of you. It wasn't that we didn't have the right to ask you to feed us, but we wanted to show you, firsthand, how you should work for your living" (3:7-9). The words "you well know" in verse 7 are in the emphatic position in the Greek. The Greek language did not always use a pronoun. Sometimes it was included in the verb itself. But here it not only is included in the verb, but a separate pronoun is added also. "You yourselves" is the real meaning. He is emphasizing the fact that "you yourselves know what to do."

SECOND THESSALONIANS 3:6-9

"Ought" is often translated "must." "You yourselves know you *must* follow our example." Paul reminds the Thessalonians of the behavior of the apostles. What they said was consistent with the lives they lived. We cannot overemphasize our practicing what we say we believe. "Do as I say, not as I do" did not work with our children, and it will not work in church either. If I tell you not to lie but lie to you, how can you believe me? If I tell you to work hard, then sit down and let others do the work, why should you listen to me? What we say has to be demonstrated in how we live. Paul is saying, "You can follow us because we preach to you what we live to you." We have no right to tell other people to do something we don't do ourselves.

"We never accepted food from anyone without buying it" (3:8). Paul didn't let someone else provide his means of living or depend on someone else to pay the bill. At this particular time in history many traveling evangelists would come in and say they were from God, but all they wanted was a free meal or would take up an offering and then leave. Paul was not like that.

"Worked hard" (3:8) comes from two strong words. When they are placed together, they give a picture of tireless and endless work to the point of exhaustion. By their example, these missionaries showed how industrious, dedicated, and disciplined these new converts were to be.

"It wasn't that we didn't have the right to ask you to feed us" (3:9). The Apostle Paul believed that the ministry had a right to be supported by the church (see 1 Cor. 9:3-14). Paul had too short a time with the Thessalonians to help them understand how they were to care for those who ministered to them. So, though he had the right to say "take care of me," for the cause of Christ and his kingdom he waived those rights.

The phrase "we wanted to show you, firsthand" literally means "to give ourselves." He says, "We literally gave ourselves as a model, an example for you to follow." This goes along with what he had said in 1 Thessalonians 2:8—"We loved you dearly—so dearly that we gave you not only God's message, but our own lives too." Paul was declaring, "We did not just preach to you—we gave you our lives. We did not just tell you God's truth—we gave you our hearts."

We must give ourselves to each other and to our world. We must give not only the Bible, but ourselves. People need to know what the Bible says, but we must give them ourselves as well.

30

The Necessity of Work
Second Thessalonians 3:10-13

In the first century, conversion to Christianity often brought calamitous consequences to the individual. Many times he would lose his job. Sometimes it was difficult for the new Christian who had broken with tradition and the ways of his community and parents to find a new one. It was quite natural that in the early Christian community there was great compassion and concern for one another. It was not uncommon for those who had much to share their goods with others. This was indeed an oasis in the desert of the pagan world, a harsh, cruel world. Christian fellowship with its love, concern, and compassion was a breath of fresh air.

And yet, one of the most beautiful virtues of the early Christian church became one of its greatest problems. Some took advantage of the generosity and love of the church. Some began to neglect their jobs, expecting others to provide for their physical needs. This centered around a doctrinal heresy and misconceptions about the second coming of Jesus Christ.

The Epistles to the Thessalonians were written primarily to combat two basic problems: misconceptions

The Necessity of Work

about the second coming, and misconceptions about the dignity of work. The pagan world thought work was an intrusion upon a person's life. It was not looked upon as something that had dignity and value, but only something one did of necessity. Even some Christians refused to work because they said, "The Lord is coming soon! Why should we work?"

"Even while we were still there with you we gave you this rule: 'He who does not work shall not eat.' Yet we hear that some of you are living in laziness, refusing to work, and wasting your time in gossiping. In the name of the Lord Jesus Christ we appeal to such people—we command them—to quiet down, get to work, and earn their own living. And to the rest of you I say, dear brothers, never be tired of doing right" (3:10-13).

THE WILL
The will is involved here. "He who does not work shall not eat" is literally, "If one chooses not to work, neither should he eat."

The word "command" (KJV) is the same word we saw earlier in this chapter. Here it is in the imperfect tense, which carries the idea of continuous action. He is saying, "We still command you that if any will not work, neither should he eat."

The Apostle Paul undertook a missionary journey to visit churches he had established, and as a part of the missionary journey he took up a collection for needy saints in Jerusalem and Judea. He was concerned for the physical needs of those who could not provide for themselves. But at the same time, he had no patience at all for someone who refused to work. He urged compassion for those who *could not* work, but not for those who *would not* work. There is no excuse for becoming a leech on society or the church. It is inconceivable that a Christian who has been redeemed by the self-sacrificing love of Jesus Christ would himself become a burden upon other Christians.

There are those today who seem to believe that the church or government owes them a living. But no one owes us a living. There is a point where Christian benevolence becomes indulgence, where we rob people of their pride by doling charity to them. By so doing we do not minister to their real need.

THE WALK
"Yet we hear that some of you are living in laziness, refusing to work, and wasting your time in gossiping" (3:11). The problem in the church at Thessalonica was not a moral one, but "laziness" or "disorderliness" (KJV). "Laziness" meant: first, refusal to work, and second, being "busybodies." In the original language, that is a play upon words. They were busy with business that was not their own. The idea is that they were going from house to house telling fantastic tales about some great revelation that had come to them about the second

coming. They were all over the community tending to everybody else's business, and at the end of the day expected somebody to feed them.

The King James Version emphasizes, "there are some which walk *among* you" (3:11). They are walking among them and yet not really participating in the fellowship of God's people.

THE WORK

"In the name of the Lord Jesus Christ we appeal to such people—we command them—to quiet down, get to work, and earn their own living" (3:12). "Such people" does not mean much to us, but it is a very tactful way of saying, "Listen, you loafers, you lazy, good-for-nothing fellows, get to work." Paul wants reconciliation, not condemnation. He is concerned that the undisciplined be brought back into the family in full fellowship, not that we cast them out. "Appeal" and "command" make an interesting combination. "Command" means, "Do it!" "Appeal" means, "Please." Paul was strong, yet gentle; emphatic, yet tender. "Appeal" comes from a root word meaning "encourage."

He tells them to "quiet down, get to work." They were too excitable. They were running around telling fantastic tales about the second coming of Jesus Christ and were in a nervous frenzy. Paul says, "I want you to work quietly." God wants each of us to have a quiet spirit and a peaceful heart. He gives us the peace that passes all understanding. Paul commands them to work quietly, with peace in their hearts, knowing that it is God's responsibility to send Jesus back and not theirs.

If I have a job to do at 8:00 A.M. and God was going to send Jesus Christ back at 8:30 A.M., he would want me to be at my desk doing my job when he comes. That is what Paul is commanding. Our task is to do what we have been assigned to do, quietly and faithfully. "Be beautiful inside, in your hearts, with the lasting charm of a gentle and quiet spirit which is so precious to God" (1 Pet. 3:4).

These people were further admonished to "earn their own living," to take care of their own needs. If we have an opportunity and can provide for ourselves, we should do it!

THE WEARINESS

"But ye, brethren, be not weary in well doing" (3:13, KJV). *The Living Bible* reveals the real intent of this verse: "never be tired of doing right." This verse is addressed to "dear brothers," not the lazy and disorderly. Paul was not making a blanket condemnation of all the church. He says, "You, my dear brothers, are doing your job. Now don't get tired of doing it. Don't let a few who have neglected their duty keep you from doing yours." It is easy for us to do that. Many do not visit. Why should we? Many do not tithe. Why should we? We must not let a few who reject their responsibility keep us from doing ours.

"Well doing" (KJV) is a word that does not appear anywhere else in the New Testament. It is a combination of two words which do appear elsewhere, but never in this combination. We are never to tire of doing that which is excellent, noble, right.

God intended for us to work. Because there is no real separation of the sacred and the secular, when we do our jobs during the week we are just as surely serving God as when we are worshiping on Sunday morning. As we work in areas outside the church, they will become sacred so that all we do will be to the glory of God. If every teacher realized that teaching children was in reality honoring and serving God, it would make a difference how he or she taught. If every lawyer looked not at the loopholes of the law, but at the responsibility that was his under God as a minister of authority, it would make a difference how he fulfilled it. If every mechanic viewed every repair job like that, it would affect how he worked. If every student saw in every class an opportunity to display the grace of God in his life, it would make a difference in the grades that were recorded and the work that was turned in. If every husband and wife saw in their home the opportunity to express the relationship that was theirs with God, it would change our homes.

Paul is saying, "Don't be weary in doing right." We are to excel in our vocations outside the church, and in our vocations in the church. This has great implications for our lives today.

31
Admonishing a Brother
Second Thessalonians 3:14-18

Second Thessalonians is a stormy book. It begins with the Apostle Paul speaking about "flaming fire," "vengeance," and "eternal destruction." In the second chapter, he talks about the "man of sin," "the one who opposes God," and how the Lord is going to come back and destroy the man of sin. It is a hard-hitting passage dealing with the Antichrist and those who follow him. Then in the third chapter, he talks about how to discipline those who are busybodies and lazy, those who are not serving God and are disrupting the fellowship of the church. This somewhat stormy epistle comes to a climax in these verses, ending with a gentle word of prayer. That's the way God is. Though he may have to rebuke us for the way we live, he still loves us and longs to give us grace and bring peace to our hearts.

"If anyone refuses to obey what we say in this letter, notice who he is and stay away from him, that he may be ashamed of himself. Don't think of him as an enemy, but speak to him as you would to a brother who needs to be warned. May the Lord of peace himself give you his peace no matter what happens. The Lord be with you all. Now here is my greeting which I am writing with my own hand, as I do at the end of all my letters, for proof that it really is from me. This is in my own handwriting. May the blessing of our Lord Jesus Christ be upon you all" (3:14-18).

CORRECTION

"If anyone refuses to obey what we say in this letter, notice who he is and stay away from him, that he may be ashamed of himself" (3:14). There is nothing more difficult than church discipline. How do we do it? When we read church history, we see that many of the abuses and great tragedies in the history of the church came out of a desire to discipline or correct those within the church who were sinful and rebellious.

"Notice" means more than just simply to realize that he is there. It is a word that originally had a rather neutral connotation. It could have reference to someone who is very good and a special note needs to be made of his goodness, or it could mean someone who is very bad and special note or awareness needs to be made of his evil. However, as the word began to be used, it came to have a very sinister connotation to it. It came to mean "evil." In Scripture and in classical Greek, the word carried the idea of marking out a wrongdoer and making an example of him as it were.

We must not ignore rebellion against God in the church. The great tragedy in the Christian church in America today is that we have so much hypocrisy, so much ungodliness, and the church has not dealt with it.

SECOND THESSALONIANS 3:14-18

The Apostle Paul is warning us of the necessity of correction for those in our fellowship who are causing disruption. Note them; do not ignore them.

Most churches never deal with this problem and even give such persons prominent positions in the church without correcting their attitude. If someone is critical, contentious, or divisive in our fellowship and we put him in a place of leadership, he will never repent and he will never help the church.

"Stay away from him" does not mean we are to kick him out. It means we are not to give him intimate fellowship and thus encourage his evil attitude. Paul does not tell us to withdraw from him to the extent that we do not love him or care about him. But he says we are not to act as if nothing has happened. We have to come to the place where we have no company with him. What Paul is saying here is an amplification of verse 6. If we never rebuke him for his divisiveness, then we are contributing to his divisiveness.

Three things in this passage must be taken together. Do not isolate any one of them. First: Mark the man. Do not act as if nothing has happened. Deal with it. Second: Have no company with him. We are not to make ourselves close friends with a person like that. Third: "That he may be ashamed of himself." "Ashamed" is a passive Greek word which gives the idea of "turning upon oneself." The idea is that if we will deal with a person like this, he will reflect upon his actions and will be led to repentance and restoration. Restoration is the purpose of discipline. We are not to condemn or look down, but to restore.

Our fellowship should be redemptive in nature. We are not to become so exclusive that we excommunicate all those who disagree with us. We are to deal with them firmly and positively, but with the thought in mind that they may be brought back into the fold. That is God's plan.

> *There is so much bad in the best of us*
> *And so much good in the worst of us*
> *That it doesn't behoove any of us to talk about the rest of us.*

When we see someone erring, can we condemn him as though there were no mercy? No, because God has placed in us a deep desire to be redemptive, encouraging, and supportive to each other.

COMPASSION
"Don't think of him as an enemy, but speak to him as you would to a brother who needs to be warned" (3:15). This is the way we are to admonish a brother, with compassion. "Do not think of him as an enemy." Before Paul tells us to encourage him as a brother, he tells us not to count him as an enemy. This is extremely important. When we have disagreements in the fellowship of the church, or when there is disobedience within the church, we do not become enemies. Too often we have forgotten who the enemy is. We are disciplining a brother—sinful, disobedient, and erring to be sure, but a brother nevertheless. There must be compassion mixed with the disci-

pline. Anyone can find fault, but it takes the spirit of Christ to restore one who is in fault.

One of the saddest things that happens in the fellowship of the church is loveless condemnation. The most vicious, mean things ever said to me have been said by church members. On the other hand, I visited at length one night with a noted atheist. That notorious atheist leader was kind to me. I despise everything she stands for, but she was gracious to me. The most vicious attacks on my ministry have come from professing Christians. The most vicious rumors that have been started about me were started by people who claim to know Christ. This ought not to be.

When there is a dissident note sounded in the fellowship, it does not make us enemies! It does not put us on opposite sides. We belong to God, and thus we belong to each other.

"Stop being mean, bad-tempered and angry. Quarreling, harsh words, and dislike of others should have no place in your lives. Instead, be kind to each other, tenderhearted, forgiving one another, just as God has forgiven you because you belong to Christ. Follow God's example in everything you do just as a much loved child imitates his father. Be full of love for others, following the example of Christ who loved you and gave himself to God as a sacrifice to take away your sins. And God was pleased, for Christ's love for you was like sweet perfume to him" (Eph. 4:31—5:2). The discipline and correction of the church must be done in love.

The word "speak" (3:15) implies encouragement. It is a word that says, "You are wrong, but I love you and I want to see you drawn back into the fellowship." The King James Version translates it "admonish."

COMMUNION
The reason we are to deal in love with those who need discipline is so we can have communion and fellowship together. "May the Lord of peace himself give you his peace no matter what happens. The Lord be with you all" (3:16). The word "all" includes the disobedient brother, the one who is rebellious. There is a communion in the fellowship of the saints that is unparalleled anywhere else in the world.

"The Lord of peace himself..." Peace comes from Jesus Christ. Peace is more than the absence of strife. It is prosperity, fullness, wholeness, happiness. We find prosperity and fulfillment in Jesus.

"The Lord of peace *himself* give you his peace." If we want peace, we will not find it anywhere but in Jesus. We will not find it in serving Jesus, but in Jesus himself. Real peace is in Jesus, not in Christian service. We have peace because Jesus Christ gave it to us in himself.

That phrase "no matter what happens" literally means "in all ways." In every circumstance of our lives, in every conceivable situation, God will give us peace. Our happiness does not depend on what happens to us. If something that happens to us takes away our joy, it should cause us to come back to our Lord with a commitment that is deep and abiding, so that our peace will depend only on him.

"The Lord be with you all." Jesus wants to be in our midst, as we draw together to deal with those who are rebellious.

Paul concludes by saying that his deep desire to communicate with those he loved led him to write the beautiful concluding greeting in his own handwriting. "May the blessing of our Lord Jesus Christ be upon you all" (3:18). The apostle's great desire was for God's grace and blessing to abound in them. As we come to recognize God as the One who can give us peace in every circumstance, his grace will abound and we shall be available for his use in a world that desperately needs the touch of Christ upon it.

Bibliography

Hastings, James. *The Great Texts of the Bible.* New York: Charles Scribner's Sons, 1914.

Hendriksen, William. *New Testament Commentary.* Grand Rapids, Mich.: Baker Book House, 1955.

Hovey, Alvah, editor. *An American Commentary on the New Testament.* Philadelphia: American Baptist Publications Society, 1887.

Morris, Leon. *The First and Second Epistles to the Thessalonians.* Grand Rapids, Mich.: Wm. B. Eerdmans Publishing Co., 1959.

Nicoll, W. Robertson. *The Expositor's Greek Testament.* Grand Rapids, Mich.: Wm. B. Eerdmans Publishing Co., 1970.

Robertson, A. T. *Word Pictures in the New Testament.* New York: Harper and Bros., 1931.

Spurgeon, C. H. *The Treasury of the Bible* (*The New Testament*). Grand Rapids, Mich.: Zondervan Publishing House, n.d.

Notes

Other resources available from Jimmy Draper

Books by Jimmy Draper
Trusting Thy Word
Faith That Works
The Last Millennium
Hebrews-The Life That Pleases God
Say, Neighbor, Your House Is On Fire

Audio Series by Jimmy Draper
Life's Greatest Satisfaction – 4 tape series
Power Of The Call – 3 tape series

For more information on these books and audio series by Jimmy Draper as well as other HeartSpring Media products, visit our website at **www.heartspringmedia.com** or contact us at:

HeartSpring Media
P.O. Box 1655
Keller, Texas 76244
1-800-856-8886